Service Level Agreements

Service Level Agreements

Measuring cost and quality in service relationships

Andrew Hiles
Director of the Kingswell Partnership of Consultants
Harwell
Oxfordshire
UK

CHAPMAN & HALL
University and Professional Division
London · Glasgow · New York · Tokyo · Melbourne · Madras

Published by Chapman & Hall, 2-6 Boundary Row, London SE1 8HN

Chapman & Hall, 2-6 Boundary Row, London SE1 8HN, UK

Blackie Academic & Professional, Wester Cleddens Road, Bishopbriggs, Glasgow G64 2NZ, UK

Chapman & Hall GmbH, Pappelallee 3, 69469 Weinheim, Germany

Chapman & Hall USA., One Penn Plaza, 41st Floor, New York, NY10119, USA

Chapman & Hall Japan, ITP - Japan, Kyowa Building, 3F, 2-2-1 Hirakawacho, Chiyoda-ku, Tokyo 102, Japan

Chapman & Hall Australia, Thomas Nelson Australia, 102 Dodds Street, South Melbourne, Victoria 3205, Australia

Chapman & Hall India, R. Seshadri, 32 Second Main Road, CIT East, Madras 600 035, India

First edition 1993
Reprinted 1994

© 1993 Andrew Hiles

Printed in Great Britain by Alden Press, Oxford

ISBN 0 412 54240 4

A Catalogue record for this book is available from the British Library
Library of Congress Cataloging-in-Publication Data available

∞ Printed on acid-free paper, manufactured in accordance with ANSI/NISO Z39.48-1992 and ANSI/NISO Z39.48-1984 (Permanence of Paper)

Contents

Preface

Frequently new technologies demand new, creative, methods of management. Occasionally these new management models have the potential to enhance the effectiveness of business areas never envisaged when the management method was originally devised: they are transferable.

One of the classic cases is the transfer of engineering management disciplines, for instance quality assurance and quality control (and more recently total quality management – TQM). Quality disciplines have permeated from the factory floor into virtually every area of corporate operations and been universally embraced by world class organizations.

Those first to seize such opportunities gain efficiency, effectiveness and, frequently, competitive edge. But all too often, organizations simply react when they see more alert competitors gaining advantage and the new techniques are implemented merely out of defence.

The opportunity to identify and adopt such new concepts at an early stage is rare: but this book presents one. The dynamic world of information services, combining explosive growth with corporate dependence, has had to create new methodologies to contain costs and manage service. One of the key methods employed by the leaders in information services management is the use of service level agreements.

While a contract will govern the legal and commercial aspects of service provision it cannot effectively govern the day-to-day delivery of the service quality – and contracts are irrelevant to in-house service providers.

Many corporate services are overheads – not profit earners, but profit dissipators. How can their cost be controlled – or better, reduced – while preserving acceptable quality?

A service level agreement is the tool which ensures delivery of consistent, appropriate and timely service quality to meet the business need at the right price.

Using case studies and examples, this book explains how service level agreements, born to meet the challenges of a new industry, can be translated as a practical management tool in any service environment, and provides a blueprint for their implementation.

Acknowledgements

Acknowledgements are due to:

- Elsevier Science Publishers Ltd for allowing me to reproduce material used in my previous book, published by Elsevier
- Mr Bill Barham, Lloyds Bank plc, for his input into the format of the standard SLA
- Mr George W.A. (Bill) Miller, American Airlines, for his excellent SLA checklist which has been adapted in this book
- Messrs John Mawhood and Chris Dering of Masons, Solicitors & Privy Council Agents, for the final Chapter.

List of figures

1

An overview of service level agreements: what they can and cannot do

1.1 Introduction

We take service departments for granted – or at least, we used to: personnel, accounts, purchasing, stores, legal, catering, training, estates, facilities management, cleaning, secretariat, engineering, public relations – all these and more may be part of our business infrastructure.

Increasingly, in-house services are seen as utility services just like electricity or water. These days, utilities world-wide are increasingly becoming privatized – expected to fund themselves as commercial entities rather than be provided by governments. But the cost of our organization's support services is increasingly questionable. Value for money is being insisted upon – but how do you measure it? Similarly, in-house services are increasingly expected to be self-sufficient, at least recovering costs from customers, rather than being provided as a corporate service as part of the overhead costs.

As with the supply of any utility, the end-user expects a defect-free service, available 100% of the time, at a reasonable cost. A utility is in direct conflict with the increasing technological or legal complexity with which the service provider has to cope in supporting perhaps a greatly increasing range of services. The service provider is often trying to cover too much ground with too few resources: he or she needs to standardize and prioritize service offerings.

Often, however, this 'utility' logic is not extended to the provision of in-house services. You know what the tariff rate is for power, gas, fuel oil and all the other utilities. The price may depend upon your negotiating power – but you know what you are getting for your money. You can measure the consumption of these services in terms of efficiency and select the appropriate quality – premium, unleaded or 4-star petrol for instance. Your organization specifies the quality it requires for any consumable that it uses. This makes sense: buying goods of a higher quality than you need wastes money. Support services are overheads – and typically it can take up to ten million pounds of sales to cover the cost of one million pounds of overheads. A look at your profit margins on turnover will illustrate this.

When the in-house service was first established, its size and scope was agreed upon. Its capacity was defined and throughput requirements may also have been stated. But there are many other aspects of the service which frequently are not quantified. Often the service requirement has not been recently checked with the customer so that changing user requirements may not be expressed in the current service specification. The service provider may be faced with increased demand and no additional resource to cover it.

All this can lead to a mismatch of expectations between the end customers and the support service provider. The end-customer perceives that the service is 'poor'. Response to requests may be 'slow'. Support may be 'patchy'. All these are unquantified – but they suggest a background noise of customer dissatisfaction with the service – especially vocal if the end-user is a paying customer. It is all too easy for the service manager to assume the customer's perception is wrong: it cannot be wrong! It is the customer's perception and will remain so until it is changed.

The service manager, being frequently more analytical than the customer, will doubtless be measuring certain aspects of the service which are perceived as key performance indicators. As long as these are at worst consistent and at best improving, the service manager may believe that a good service is being provided.This service may not, however, be what the customer wants! So how do we align the service to the needs of its customers?

1.2 Service level agreements: definition

Service level agreements were first developed for in-house service providers (the pioneers were the computing services). External services are usually dealt with by contracts which may specify service level requirements. However, many contracts for external services are vague in service terms and in some cases a service level agreement may supplement a contract.

A service level agreement is simply:

> 'an agreement between the service provider and its customers quantifying the minimum acceptable service to the customer.'

Each of these words is important. A service level agreement (SLA) takes the form 'if you do this, then I will be able to do that, and this will be the cost'. It has to be negotiated and **agreed**. Agreement is two-way. It depends on the customer providing accurate utilization and volume forecasts (perhaps not exceeding n transactions per hour) and in the customer meeting deadlines (say for providing a consistent volume of work to the service provider, or for not exceeding a peak demand limit). As with any negotiation each side will start out with an opening position. This position will be modified as negotiations continue, to take account of practical difficulty and cost. This negotiation should not be some sort of duel between the service professional and the customer: it should be a joint exploration of what is in the best interests of the customer's business. For in-house service providers it is also their business.

Quantifying the service is vital. There is an old saying 'what can't be measured doesn't exist'. Quantification of various aspects of the service will place assessment of its quality on an objective basis and get away from those vague, emotive words like 'slow' and 'poor'.

The service specification should be the **minimum** service level acceptable as meeting the customer requirement. The end customer or end user's requirement will be examined to establish what the benefits of various levels of service are and what level is cost justified. There is probably no benefit in over-providing quality: it just costs more money. Over-provision of quality – for instance by providing a one-hour turnround when there is spare capacity – may just raise expectations to a level which becomes unsupportable later when the workload increases and that initial quality cannot be maintained. The service has to be fully adequate but it needs to be more than that. However, the quality must also be consistent since inconsistent quality is equated to poor quality by the customer.

The definition of **minimum** (that is, adequate) has to be explored. The pyramid model of service and value (Figure 1.1) may help in this process. This model identifies four levels of service from Level Zero (the customers are on their own, without support from the service provider) to Level Four (highest quality service).

Level Zero may apply to areas where customer expertise exceeds that of the service supplier, or to non-critical areas. Level Four may apply to mission critical or high-value services. In general, the higher the level of service, the higher is the service cost and the lower the risk of loss of service: the lower the level, the cheaper the service but the greater is the risk of loss of service. In presenting multiple options of levels of service, management is prompted to establish the quality of service appropriate to that area. This process defines the minimum service requirement.

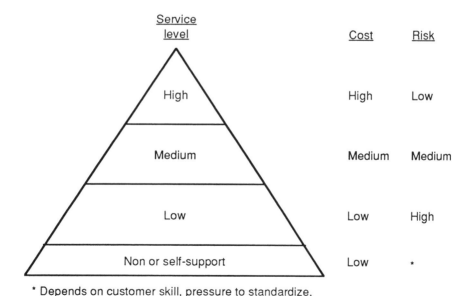

* Depends on customer skill, pressure to standardize, value of the service on the business.

Figure 1.1   Service support characteristics.

Thus if a support service consistently meets the minimum standard its service level will be perceived by the customer as good. If it over-achieves that does not necessarily mean a better service: it may just mean a more expensive service.

Minimum also applies to the range of services offered. Does the customer need a choice of three types of restaurant service and 12 main courses, 250 stock stationery items, four different word-processing packages, three similar training courses? The more options we clog our services with, the more the service costs – in capacity, in external spend and in support effort. So we need to establish the minimum range of facilities we should be offering.

The service has to be **acceptable** to the customer. Customers have their jobs to do and the support services only exist to help them to do it. Many companies are undergoing a fundamental change of perception about their internal service providers and business units. Particularly if a support service is charged out, 'customer' is a more appropriate word than 'user' of a service. In this case, the SLA may also need to contain charge-out terms. In any event, users of support services are our customers – so let us treat them as such.

That is another benefit of an SLA: it promotes customer orientation within the support services.

Yes, our customers have their job to do, but why? Many of them may themselves be in other service departments. If we only exist to serve our customers, why do our customers exist? Their role is to support the business mission – to sell widgets, to implement legislation, to bill customers so as to provide timely cashflow, in short to service our organizational goal, whatever that is.

1.3 Serving the business

Every organization has a mission. Public authorities exist to provide certain defined services and their political masters may dictate the quality and cost criteria to which those services are to be provided. Commercial undertakings exist to provide profits for their shareholders by providing certain products or services. Every successful business has a clear understanding of its role, often defined in a mission statement. This is backed up by a corporate strategy, by a five-year plan, a three-year plan and detailed annual business targets. The corporate plan is supported by business analysis which specifies the support services required and by senior management setting departmental objectives. Individual departments within the organization then set their own:

- mission statement
- strategy
- five-year plans
- three-year plans
- business analysis
- system specification
- departmental annual targets
- individual objectives for their staff.

Departments and staff can then deliver their contribution to the corporate mission. Corporate achievement of its targets is thus a sort of project, with a series of deliverables against deadlines and milestones. Each department (and each member of staff) has to be considered 'contracted' to produce specified deliverables if the corporate plan is to be achieved. Where these departments rely on a support service, the service should be 'subcontracted' internally or to an external supplier, to provide that support at appropriate capacity, quality and cost. An SLA represents this 'subcontract' with an in-house support service or amplifies a contract for an external service.

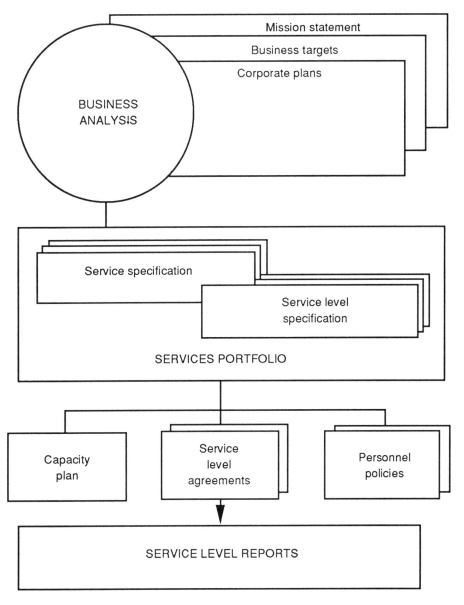

Figure 1.2 Serving the business.

An SLA therefore orients the support service to the business plan – and pre-empts situations where the service tail wags the organizational dog or where a service empire is allowed to grow up without quantification of its real contribution to the business (Figure 1.2)

1.4 Quality Standards ISO 9004 Part 2

Quality management criteria are laid down in ISO 9001–9004. Of these the most relevant is the new draft standard ISO 9004 Part 2 'Guidelines for Services'. Using this as a guide we might wish to specify a number of parameters for a service that might be included in an SLA:

- facilities, capacity, number of personnel, quantity of stores;
- waiting time, delivery time, process times;
- hygiene, safety, reliability, security;
- responsiveness, accessibility, courtesy, comfort, aesthetics of environment, competence, dependability, accuracy, completeness, state of the art, credibility, communication.

1.5 Availability

Service level agreements work to identify appropriate service parameters for the support service. The most obvious of these parameters is service availability.

What do we mean by availability? Is it simply the opening hours of the travel claims section? Or do we mean a total service? That is do we include everything to do with business travel – flight information, visas, passport renewal, flight bookings, rail ticket reservations, hotel bookings, transfers, car hire, travel insurance, foreign currency imprests, vaccinations, inoculations? And is availability defined solely at head office or do we include every single intermediate step to getting the tickets into the traveller's hands? Airlines, insurers, couriers, baggage handlers, car hire firms, taxis – should the SLA include them, too? Do we measure availability at head office – or in the customer's – the business traveller's – hands?

In short, do we include all the components and all the delivery mechanisms used to provide the total service or just those judged to be critical? Where alternative services or delivery mechanisms exist, should availability be taken to mean the availability of at least one service or one delivery mechanism? Similarly, where there are multiple points of service delivery – say several booking offices for rail tickets – is the service 'available' despite one or more of the booking offices being closed? And if, instead of being provided with Club Class tickets we can only book Economy, is that an 'available' service?

And what about downstream customers, accessing our service perhaps via agents or via computers which are part of other external networks: they may complain of our unavailability, but that unavailability may be due to a problem with the agent or to the malfunction of a computer service within an external network.

In a 'utility' environment, the supplier usually has well defined 'end points' or 'service points'. SLAs should specify these.

Even if all the physical components of the service are running, there may be a resource problem – say staff off sick – which impacts on the service and prevents all or some customers from using it. At what stage does that fault make the service 'un-available'? If one customer is affected? What if the customer can access some, but not all, of the parts of the service – if there is plenty of soup, but no main course?

Reliability can be considered part of availability: an analogy with the availability of a machine may help to illustrate the point. An availability target expressed in terms of percentage uptime could conceal poor reliability with numerous short breaks. And if every time you call on your site engineer there is a notice on the door saying 'back in five minutes' the engineer is effectively unavailable. The number and duration of service outages is therefore also a significant indicator of the quality of availability.

A definition of 'availability' that is valid for any particular support service – or for a particular group of customers – can only be established by exploring these issues with customers. In general, however, the customer tends increasingly to be inter-ested in availability to them at their workplace (on their desk or in their hands) at all times they are accustomed to receiving it. As far as the customer is concerned, the service is unavailable if he or she cannot access it – and the actual location or cause of the fault does not affect this perception!

The corollary of this is that, if the customer has not wanted to access the service, he doesn't perhaps care whether it is available or not. So availability also needs to be defined in terms of 'when'. A lower level of availability may be adequate overnight, or at weekends or bank holidays for some services. Availability requirements during normal working hours – say 0900 hours to 1700 hours – may be substantially higher than outside normal working hours.

Equally, there may be critical periods where even the availability targets for nor-mal working hours are inadequate: for financial staff near period- or year-end, for salary payrolls at month-end, for retail point-of-sale support services immediately before Christmas and Easter. Critical periods may be different for each system, for each major customer or for each group of users.

Not just availability, but the appropriate quality of the available service needs to be established.

In short, 'availability' needs defining by each component of the service and by each dependency or link. Having defined 'availability' in terms of the components or links and in terms of critical times, other service parameters need addressing.

1.6 Performance: speed, response and accuracy

Job turnround may be an important factor – requests for service and the input as-sociated with that request may have to be completed by a specific time and certain support service activities may have to be actioned within a timeframe or completed to meet the deadline. For instance, an electrician service may be asked to provide addi-tional power or heating for a specific event – say a conference or promotional event. Targets for turnround and deadline therefore need to be established.

Speed by itself is of little use – speed needs to be accompanied by appropriate ac-curacy. The old question 'do you want it now, or do you want it right?' is appropriate here: often speed will reduce accuracy. It is a two-way process – the service supplier can often only deliver if the customer provides input to a certain quality or accuracy. If drafts for a secretarial service are illegible or financial information submitted to an accounts department is incomplete, it is unrealistic to expect that support service to complete to a deadline, particularly where data is input to a system manually. Accuracy levels and quality of input therefore also need to be specified – particularly where meeting deadlines and throughput targets may depend on the accuracy of the customer's input.

For many support services, response is an important quality criterion. Certain jobs may need to be completed within a defined time. This will vary with the type of service and will depend on whether the customer's routine function is dependent on the support service. It is pointless, for instance, for an estates function to provide information on new premises so tardily that the premises have already been sold to a competitor. To take another example: a slower telephone response may be acceptable for booking delegates on training courses than for currency arbitrage.

Response costs money. In the Big Bang (the relaxation of the securities and financial services markets in the UK), stockbrokers Kleinwort Grieveson in the UK specified the maximum computer terminal response time for 400 trading desks at five seconds. The initial project cost was £12 million: to reduce response time to one second would have cost a further £24 million! The parallel with other services is clear. To get a service desk to answer calls within ten seconds may take, say, five staff. To improve the responsiveness to a guaranteed five second answer time might take ten staff – and involve high staff levels just to cover peak periods and long slack periods of unproductive 'idle time' for staff out of peak hours.

1.7 Security

Equally, security may be a significant issue – in a corporate strategy, Research and Development, audit or a personnel function for instance. An SLA will need to establish relevant security criteria in terms of physical and logical access to the support service, its files, data and output as well as providing for business continuity and contingency plans.

1.8 Quality: process control

Service quality covers more than just those items mentioned above. Sometimes SLAs have been introduced to enforce compliance with quality assurance and quality control standards – as part of a zero-defect approach. If SLAs set high quality standards the support service has to deliver them – or lose credibility.

The control of service and service delivery to such parameters can usually only be achieved by controlling the process that delivers the service. Process performance measurement and control are therefore essential to achieve and maintain the required service quality. If quality defects are not discovered until final inspection, it is probably too late.

The service delivery process may range from the highly automated (like a telephone call) to the highly personalized (like legal, medical or consultancy services). The more definable the process, whether by automation or by detailed procedures, the easier it is to apply structured quality disciplines.

1.9 Service products

What are the support services we provide? Not generically, like accounting, but specifically what are the service products within that generic area? Accounts receivable, modelling, travel claims, accounts payable, management information, payroll, provision of annual accounts, budget information, project budget, forecast financial out-turns, unit costs ... and many more. By looking at each service product, we can fine-tune service delivery. There has to be a finite limit to the service products which can be provided from a fixed resource. Identify service products and we can then prioritize and perhaps rationalize them.

1.10 Points of delivery and delivery mechanisms

But we also need to define to what points the service should be delivered and by what means it should be delivered to those points. Is it a walk-in service, or do we aim to support customers at their desks? If at their desks, is it by physically visiting them, by documentary correspondence, by computer system or by telephone?

1.11 Service culture

The responsiveness of central support services may typically lag behind the needs of the customer of those services. Historically, there may be backlog mountains where worthy but relatively minor service requests have been pushed to the bottom of the priority pile. Some central functions got the reputation of telling their customers what they could have rather than providing what was needed. Others tended to be technology led or led by current developments in their profession rather than solution led, perhaps providing 'Rolls-Royce' solutions when the business need was for something cheaper and less sophisticated. And however much a service has improved, customer expectations tend to improve more quickly.

Yet other support services have never declared service targets. They have missed deadlines and targets required (but perhaps not specified) by customers. Thus the support services have consequently suffered a reputation for poor service. This may have been because the two-way nature of the service was not fully appreciated: the support service may only be able to deliver against service targets if the customer delivers against agreed input delivery, accuracy and volume targets.

Many support functions do not hold service review meetings with their customers at all. But where service review meetings do take place against this background, they tend to degenerate into bitter and personalized affairs: in the absence of objective performance criteria, individuals are blamed for failing to do their job properly.

It was against this background – mainly in a computing environment – that SLAs were originally designed. They imposed a commitment on both sides – on the computing service to provide a defined service and on the customer to be committed to using that service within defined parameters. This depersonalized the service review meetings and led to objective assessment of performance by both parties.

Their success in the information technology area led to experiments with SLAs in other areas. Often SLAs have been introduced as a means of forcing service management techniques on a support service lacking these professional methods.

They have also been seized upon as a tool to encourage – impose even – a service orientation on the support services. SLAs facilitate a service culture. They establish targets and commit the support service – and customers – to deliver them.

This is particularly true when the organization is considering internal charging for services: where internal users are, for the first time, having to budget and pay for services these internal customers have a right to a clear definition of the quality of service they are buying.

1.12 But why SLAs?

A number of arguments can be brought against SLAs:

- *The service was originally subject to a justification. This justification should have laid down service criteria.* (True, but how many actually did? Besides, the business changes, life changes, volumes change, values change and a historical justification may not be valid a year later.)
- *Our staff are professional: we can motivate them to deliver service without SLAs.* (Yes, but don't SLAs help by defining objective targets?)
- *SLAs confine service to the minimum.* (That is the point of them – to the minimum acceptable level.)
- *You do not need SLAs to introduce charge-out of service.* (No, but the customer is entitled to know exactly what he or she is paying for – and how to measure whether they are getting it.)
- *If service management methodologies are in place, who needs SLAs?* (OK, so **you** know you're doing a professional job. How does the customer know?)
- *Why generate SLA overheads?* (Quality and control have a cost. However, the shape of the SLA selected need not be the one with the heaviest overheads – pick the right one for your organization.)
- *Who is going to believe the service provider if they are doing the monitoring of performance against SLAs?* (Customers are quite capable of seeing through phoney figures – and customers should be doing some of the monitoring themselves.)
- *Why not just issue a brochure describing the service? That is what the electricity and gas providers do.* (Fine – but if you cover every service aspect with service targets you are effectively writing an SLA without imposing any reciprocal agreement on customers to enable the service provider to meet those targets. What controls demand? Until recently many utilities have been publicly owned and demand driven, but now they are having to tailor service far more.)

- *We have quality management already.* (SLAs are part of quality management – how can you manage quality without defining the service?)

None of these arguments destroys the fundamental logic behind SLAs.

SLAs force the support service to orient itself to providing cost-effective service solutions to business needs and to support the business plan. They impel management decisions on the appropriate quality of service to be provided. They correct ivory tower astigmatism, directing the vision away from technological or professional issues of the service provider and into a business perspective.

SLAs may sound like a universal panacea – but there are a number of things an SLA cannot do. An SLA cannot compensate for inadequate definition of business objectives, nor can it compensate for lack of standards. SLAs cannot substitute for poor customer management or poor support service management. They do not obviate the need for other service management disciplines and tools. They cannot be implemented without cost, nor be implemented without resource. Most importantly, they cannot be effective without commitment from both customer and service provider.

Both parties need to deliver their parts of the SLA – the quality of service can only be as good as the accuracy of the customer's forecast usage and the customer's adherence to their part of the agreement.

To see how well prepared your organization is to implement SLAs, complete Checklist 1. You may also wish to amend Checklist 1 to use as a quality audit document.

Checklist 1: Service orientation

	Yes	No
1. Do formal service management procedures exist to manage:		
• service levels?	☐	☐
• capacity to provide service?	☐	☐
• availability of the service?	☐	☐
• service performance?	☐	☐
• problems?	☐	☐
• changes:		
– to the technology?	☐	☐
– in legislation?	☐	☐
– in staffing?	☐	☐
– in other areas impacting on service provision?	☐	☐
• operational procedures?	☐	☐
• security (if appropriate)?	☐	☐
• environmental aspects impacting on service provision?	☐	☐
2. Are these formally documented and:		
• reviewed periodically (e.g. six-monthly)?	☐	☐
• subject to formal change procedure when new procedures, technology, legislation etc. are brought in?	☐	☐
• is documentation available to line management and are all sections involved in providing the service to customer support management and staff?	☐	☐

	Yes	No
• issued automatically to new incumbents of these posts on arrival?	☐	☐
• are end-users (customers) aware of them?	☐	☐
3. Do service level agreements exist for all support services?		
4. Do they cover all service products?	☐	☐
5. And all customers?	☐	☐
6. Do these service level agreements specify:		
• customer workload in business units (e.g. number of invoices produced)?	☐	☐
• forecast changes over the duration of the agreement?	☐	☐
• customer workload in terms of performance and capacity requirement?	☐	☐
• peak workload?	☐	☐
• peak workload constraints to limit peak capacity?	☐	☐
• security?	☐	☐
• business continuity and contingency planning?	☐	☐
• key records needed for recovery?	☐	☐
• arrangements for monitoring customer satisfaction?	☐	☐
• reports of actual service delivery against service targets:		
– for support service management?	☐	☐
– for customers?	☐	☐
7. Are service level targets included in project specifications, new product specifications, business forecasts, etc.?	☐	☐
8. Are they included in service and equipment purchase and maintenance contracts?	☐	☐
9. Are they included as part of the checklist before new products or commercial services are launched?	☐	☐
10. Is there a formal sign-off stage at which the support service provider accepts new technology as a production system?	☐	☐
11. Is there a formal sign-off stage at which the end-user (customer) accepts that new support services are meeting service level requirements?	☐	☐
12. Is service performance checked against the service requirement specification at post implementation reviews?	☐	☐
13. Are service level targets set by the support service provider:		
• for each type of usage (e.g. telephone enquiry, search, response to correspondence, etc.)?	☐	☐
• for each regime (e.g. normal working day, extended working day, overnight, weekend, bank holiday)?	☐	☐
14. If so, are they published to their customers?	☐	☐
15. Are customers committed to forecast their utilization?	☐	☐
16. And keep to their forecasts?	☐	☐
17. Do service level objectives form part of the support service job descriptions and targets for management by objectives (MBO)?	☐	☐
18. Is the support service charged out?	☐	☐
19. If so:		
• are rebates given to customers for failure to achieve service level objectives?	☐	☐

	Yes	No
• and are any penalties applied if customers exceed utilization forecasts?	☐	☐
20. Has a customer satisfaction survey been issued within the last six months?	☐	☐
21. If so, does it give scope for customer response on adequacy of service levels?	☐	☐
22. And is the service level perceived as:		
• better than 12 months ago?	☐	☐
• worse than 12 months ago?	☐	☐
• constant?	☐	☐
23. Are service level review meetings regularly held with customers to review actual achievement against service level targets?	☐	☐
24. Are utilization and performance statistics provided to assist this review?	☐	☐
25. Is performance measurement 'in the customer's hands'?	☐	☐
26. Do support service staff know the value of their customer's work:		
• in terms of percentage volume of, or income to, the support service?	☐	☐
• in terms of value to and impact on the business in the event of the support service not being provided?	☐	☐
27. Are the relative priorities of each support service product established:		
• for performance?	☐	☐
• for priority of action in the event of resource shortage or lack of full availability of the support service?	☐	☐
28. Does each support service have a designated and documented owner?	☐	☐
29. Has one person been nominated as responsible for all day-to-day aspects of the provision of that support service product?	☐	☐
30. Do customers have a single point of contact within the support service for any queries, complaints or problems about the service (e.g. a help desk)?	☐	☐
31. Is this single point of contact documented and promulgated to customers?	☐	☐
32. Is there a single point of contact in the customer area for the support service regarding service queries?	☐	☐
33. Is the single point of contact documented and promulgated within the support service?	☐	☐
34. Are all customer problems (even 'trivial' problems) logged?	☐	☐
35. Is a formal, documented escalation procedure in place for customer problems?	☐	☐
36. And is it promulgated to all relevant support service staff and to customers?	☐	☐
37. Are support service responsibilities unambiguously defined, documented and promulgated so that this single point of contact knows who, within the support service, to approach to resolve any query, complaint or problem which arises?	☐	☐
38. For each support service product:		
• is there an inventory of equipment and tools needed to provide and deliver it?	☐	☐

	Yes	No
• is there a configuration diagram showing dependencies, interrelated equipment and support service products?	☐	☐
39. Are customer problems interfaced to support service problem management procedures within the support service (e.g. progress-chasing of suppliers etc.)?	☐	☐
40. Are customer problems interfaced to support service change management procedures?	☐	☐
41. Is change management procedure extended to all changes – including documentation and personnel?	☐	☐
42. Are there back-to-back service level agreements with other internal and external suppliers on whom the support service relies to provide the service?	☐	☐
43. Are formal quality assurance and quality control procedures in place?	☐	☐
44. Are zero-defect goals in place?	☐	☐

2

The measurement of service availability and quality: key metrics and techniques which may be used

2.1 Introduction

Service availability and quality metrics have been pioneered in the information technology world and other service providers can learn something from the metrics which have been adopted by computing services.

To deliver a service which truly satisfies our customers, we need to reduce interruptions of service to a minimum. To do this we need methodologies in place for the management of service availability.

2.2 Service availability

Service availability management techniques have to be in place for the day-to-day running of our services. These services may be:

- central (for example a service provided by, say, a single head office location to a number of customers or sites);
- distributed (perhaps services provided locally on a number of different sites);
- background (that is those services which are not especially time critical – perhaps they may be completed overnight or out of normal peak periods);
- real-time (those services which require instant response – for instance, telephone directory enquiries);
- support (those services ancillary to the main service provided – perhaps a help line, training or documentation).

The effective delivery of these services depends upon the resources which are in place. These resources may be:

- plant (e.g. printing equipment, canteen equipment, cleansing equipment, or whatever other plant is required to deliver the service);
- environment/space (accommodation to deliver the service including perhaps lighting, power supplies, air conditioning, a clean-room environment – that is accommodation to an appropriate specification and size to enable the service provider effectively to operate);
- computer systems (hardware, telecommunications and networks, software);
- people (of the appropriate expertise and experience);
- finance (to fund service provision to the appropriate quality).

Defined services, using specified resources, have to be delivered to particular objectives. The objectives may be framed in terms of:

- availability (the days and times over which the service is to be provided and the length of time over which a defect-free service is to be provided);
- performance (the responsiveness and accuracy of the service);
- capacity (the mean and peak throughput requirements);
- security (the level of privacy, confidentiality, integrity and the disciplines required of the service so that it can continue to function in the event of various disaster scenarios);
- quality (the degree of support provided by the service and the acceptable defect level of the service).

Service availability suffers most, not from the routine, but from abnormal events. The two most important disciplines required in order to provide continuity of service – high availability – are probably management of:

- change, and
- problems.

Figure 2.1 shows the relationship of the service management methodologies to service level reporting.

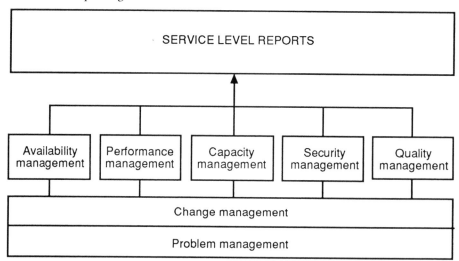

Figure 2.1   Service level reports and service management.

2.3 Change management

One of the most common causes for lack of service availability is poor change management.

Change management is normally thought of in a production or information technology context. However, change management is equally applicable to all services. Change management needs to control the movement of a service from conception through the various stages of creation and development to its acceptance as an operational service and finally to its acceptance by customers as a usable and useful service. Change needs to be consciously managed and all too often the formal operational and customer acceptance stages are omitted. The penalties for omitting these vital steps are that the organization may be left with a fragile service, the frequent loss of which can impact not only on its customers but also on the reputation of the organization – perhaps causing the loss of credibility or even costing business. Even if this is not the case, unless those responsible for operating a production service have had the opportunity to become committed to it by accepting it, unless it has been tested, at least as a pilot, under various permutations and with the demand and volumes likely to arise, then the service may fail when it is actually put into use.

One of the main problems of service provision is in unleashing a demand which the service does not have the resource or the capacity to handle. Where there is any uncertainty about the demand levels, therefore, marketing disciplines should come into play. The market should be segmented so that initially the service is offered only to a market segment with which optimistic demand forecasts indicate that the resource and capacity level is adequate to deal. Only after this pilot stage should the service be extended gradually so that resource and capacity can be adjusted to match demand.

Service level agreements are discussed within a creative or development context in Chapter 3. But quality – especially in terms of service availability and performance requirements – should be built into the design and planning of the service and should be one of the criteria upon which a decision is made whether or not to offer the service in a production environment.

The same is true of enhancement or modifications to existing services. A formal change of procedures needs to be applied and acceptance of the modified services into production working should include service level aspects.

In concept all new services, enhancements or modifications should be subject to change control procedures and formalized acceptance into production mode.

Change procedures should be applied not only to the marketing or contractual aspects but also to plant, documentation and even to procedural, organizational and personnel changes as well as to changes of key suppliers (including maintenance). Incorrect or ambiguous documentation – for instance on how to operate plant, hardware or software or on how to apply for benefits – can effectively cause the service to be unavailable just as easily as catastrophic failure of plant. This principle applies to organizational change which could leave key support functions uncovered and to personnel change which could lead to a loss of key areas of expertise. Establishing new contracts with suppliers and changing suppliers could result in service outage and unavailability of material or of essential services.

2.4 Problem management

Problems may hit the availability of the service or responsiveness of the service. Unless the problem is properly managed the period of unavailability or poor response can be protracted – indeed it can almost become a way of life and may eventually become reluctantly tolerated by the customer. There therefore needs to be a clear procedure for reporting problems to a central point within the services area (e.g. a help desk), for problems to be logged, prioritized and pursued through to resolution with appropriate escalation procedures. It is important to note that all problems should be logged – even trivial ones. The easily resolved, apparently trivial problems may indicate an undercurrent of customer irritation at the service which can readily be addressed by a simple solution such as additional training or better documentation.

Lack of availability of the service means that something has gone wrong: in order to improve service availability, we need to conduct a thorough problem audit of the service, learning from things that have gone wrong in the past and identifying weak spots and vulnerable targets so that we can improve the resilience of the service being provided.

If the database of problems is maintained, searches can be made of problems related to particular aspects of the service, to specific items of equipment or to specific services, and this will aid problem audit.

2.5 Critical component analysis

One method of conducting this audit is through critical component analysis.

Any service depends on a number of components – which, in this context, can be defined to include people, knowledge, documentation, equipment, telecommunications, accommodation, power and consumables.

Unavailability of the entire service may be caused by the loss of a single component. To provide a consistent availability of service, therefore, we need to examine vulnerability to the loss of any of the components upon which our service relies and to build in robustness or alternatives.

A critical component can be defined as: a path, piece of equipment, material, item of computer hardware or software, knowledge, a supplied support service or a person without which the service would be unable to function.

During SLA negotiations with customers, availability targets can be defined and the need for improved availability management is likely to emerge. The ways in which customers use the service will need to be analysed so that the criticality of components in that way of use or access path can initially be determined, and subsequently monitored. To improve service availability, these critical components need to be identified and resilience has to be put into place.

Availability of **all** components in the chain needs to be considered, since improvement of resilience of the most obvious critical component might simply reveal another criticality further downstream. Critical component failure analysis needs to be undertaken of:

- local equipment

- telecommunications dependencies
- central equipment
- plant
- supporting computer hardware
- supporting computer software
- supporting computer databases
- support staff
- procedures and documentation
- supplied services
- personnel
- transport and delivery mechanisms
- special consumables.

Typically, weak spots may be:

- inadequate resource
- inadequate cover in event of holidays or sickness (for instance lack of cross training or head-count restraints)
- plant or equipment subject to high breakdown levels
- supplied services subject to interruption
- undocumented procedures, processes or systems
- dependence on an unreliable intermediary.

For each area it is necessary to establish the actual availability of the critical components and to seek answers to fundamental questions:

- Who owns the component (for example, does the service provider own it or does the customer own it)?
- Who should 'own it' (in the sense of accepting responsibility for its availability)?
- What is its mean time to fail (or mean time between failures – MTBF)?
- How many times has it been unavailable in the last one, three and six month periods?
- At what times?
- What is its percentage theoretical availability during:
  - 'normal office hours' expected by customers?
  - a couple of hours either side of that?
  - weekends or other periods when it may not always be required?
- Is that the percentage availability to the customer of that component?
- If not, what was preventing the customer from using it during that theoretical availability (i.e. was there another critical component which failed downstream)?
- What did that service outage cost the business?
- What is its mean time to fix (MTTF)?
- Are there any alternatives to that component?
- How can alternatives or resilience be built in?
- At what cost?
- What would the absence of this component cost per hour/day/week in a worst case scenario?

The answers to these questions will enable the customer and service provider to establish what (if any) spend is reasonable to improve availability to the service level preferred by the customer.

Availability management may be provided in some cases simply by having staff available on call-out or by keeping a spare component (e.g. a spare valve) or by improving the maintenance call-out arrangements.

2.6 Relationship with security and contingency planning

At this stage the lines between availability management, security, risk management and contingency planning become blurred.

In establishing the appropriate service levels for an SLA, it may be necessary to modify existing security or contingency planning arrangements. It may equally be necessary to reduce some of the present risks which the service provider faces.

One step on from the critical component failure analysis is the approach taken by the Swedish Vulnerability Board, Stockholm. Their 'security by analysis' risk methodologies can equally be applied to maintaining availability targets.

The Swedish Vulnerability Board's approach is broken down into a number of separate areas, and has been adapted below to apply to a broad range of services.

2.6.1 Start

This methodology is one of identifying risks. These risks may be external or internal. Such a risk analysis is a prerequisite for a business continuity and contingency plan and should in any event be undertaken by any organization. It may reveal areas where risk can be reduced and hence the probability of availability increased.

2.6.2 Dependence

This stage examines corporate reliance on the service and the extent of the organization's exposure in the event of its failure.

2.6.3 Service

This phase examines each service and includes the equivalent of the critical component failure analysis approach.

2.6.4 Scenario

The scenario stage examines the current security arrangements and looks at a number of 'what if' situations by which the service might become unavailable.

2.6.5 Action plans

Action plans are prepared to enhance the probability of the service being available. This concept is similar to that depicted in Figure 1.1 in Chapter 1. These plans are at three levels: maximum availability (which may imply highest cost); medium availability (which usually implies more moderate cost); and low (the minimum required at the lowest cost). It then becomes a management decision as to which of these action plans is to be implemented.

2.6.6 Output

The output stage provides ongoing assessment and monitoring procedures.

2.6.7 Project

Security by analysis is a technique to identify security weaknesses; this technique may be applied to risks in the development of key new services from the conception of these new services.

2.6.8 Service development

Checklist items are included to cover the resilience and security of services as they are being developed.

2.6.9 Key personnel

A methodology is provided to identify key personnel and assess what cover is available in the event of their absence.

2.6.10 The auditor

A comprehensive guide for auditors is part of the approach and auditors are encouraged to look at the security and continuity aspects of the service.

2.6.11 Legislation

The final area provides a framework whereby existing and new legislation is summarized and service procedures and service provision are compared with the requirements of that legislation to assess whether or not they conform to it.

Whatever the method, a security risk management and contingency planning review is recommended before embarking on SLAs. The present position has to be identified so that arrangements can be compared to the customer's requirements which will be established as part of the SLA negotiations. Quality service can only be delivered if security management disciplines are in place.

2.7 Scope of service

Most services can be broken down into a number of service elements or subsidiary services. Of these, what are the SLAs going to cover? What will be the hours of service? A full SLA will cover many areas, but will usually include:

- providing information about services offered;
- taking the order;
- provision and delivery of each type of service:
  - real-time services
  - background services (less time-critical)
  - distributed or remote services;
- points of service delivery;
- help desk and technical support;
- security services (emergency requirements);
- peak period requirements;
- special requirements;
- documentation;
- subcontracts;
- training;
- billing and collecting payment.

2.8 Service hours

The SLA needs to specify the hours when service will be available. Allowance will need to be made for scheduled unavailability. Scheduled unavailability may include:

- preventative maintenance of plant and equipment or for enhancement of computer software;
- equipment change;
- staffing training;
- equipment testing and installation;
- environmental work, building maintenance, etc.

The timing of scheduled service outages can best be decided by surveying the customer's critical periods and seeking to minimize any impact on them. Whenever possible, scheduled outages should take place out of normal working hours. This will have a cost in overtime rates for the work to be done which needs to be balanced against the cost of the outage to the organization.

The times of regular scheduled outages (e.g. preventative maintenance) should be published as part of the SLA, and in service guides.

As much notice as possible should be given of any changes to service hours unless urgent work is required: at least 48 hours' notice for minor changes and perhaps a month for major changes.

Some services may be provided unmanned (e.g. by answerphone, voice response system, or automated entry access control systems). Consideration needs to be given to the impact of failure during periods of unmanned service. Most disasters (and the most expensive ones) happen over the weekend. It may be necessary to invest in intelligent environmental monitoring systems – software usually running on a personal computer to which all warning and alarm systems are connected (fire, water and intruder detection systems, air conditioning, plant monitoring, etc.). Typically such a system would have an uninterruptible power supply and would take remedial action such as invoking call-out arrangements and telephoning on-call staff or emergency services.

A differentiation may need to be made between service levels during manned operation and unmanned operation and between technical and customer support service levels – for instance a help desk – in normal working hours and outside of normal working hours.

Since groups of customers will have different working periods, cover may be required during an extended working day (perhaps from 0800 hours to 1900 hours) to cater for overtime working by the customer. Services to senior management, to the leisure industries, and to the catering and hotel trades may be particularly demanding.

Service levels need to reflect achievable targets and realistic allowances need to be made for problems arising during unmanned periods.

2.9 Real-time services

The standard hours of availability for real-time services need to be established. Availability targets should be set for these standard hours with, perhaps, a lesser target for services outside of those hours.

Response times for real-time services need to be set and the keynote should be consistency of response. It may, however, be advisable to set longer response times for peak periods and to explain to customers that response will vary according to workload. Workload limits can be set beyond which the response cannot be guaranteed.

It may be useful to set response times not for an individual transaction (for instance, time from receiving an order for a hamburger to giving the hamburger to the customer) but in terms of a 'basket' of transactions (hamburger, french fries, coffee). This helps to smooth out the occasional aberration on a single type of transaction.

Real-time transactions can be broken down into different categories with individual targets – for instance '90% of transaction type 1 to be completed within one minute'.

Particular care should be taken when setting targets for complex services: customers may make demands without appreciating the resources these use and they may have unrealistic expectations of response times from the service for such demands. Limitations on response time targets should be clearly established. Similarly, availability targets have to allow, where appropriate, for peak periods where there may be heavy competition for a given resource.

2.10 Background services

Standard schedules for background work need to be established (e.g. 'films handed in by 1000 hours will be processed and prints ready for collection by 1600 hours'). It should be made clear that processing schedules can only be kept if the customer adheres to agreed deadlines to submit input to the system. Equally, volumes of input need to be specified above which it may not be possible to maintain the schedule.

Accuracy requirements may also need to be stated: a high level of illegible orders could result in a substantial error or order reject rate and consequently missed delivery targets.

Arrangements for handover of input from the customer to the service provider should be specified together with authorization procedures. Any run-to-run controls should also be identified.

2.11 Administrative services

There has been talk of the paperless office for well over a decade and most organizations are little nearer to it. However, negotiating administrative service level agreements provides the opportunity to question the reasons why many organizations become buried under paper. It gives the opportunity to establish the validity of many administrative processes.

2.11.1 Timeliness

If financial reports on project management, for instance, are not produced until after the project is completed, they are of little use to the project manager! This analogy can be carried into many other areas: in many cases, unless information is produced at the right time its value rapidly diminishes – in some cases it may not be worthwhile producing the information at all.

2.11.2 Relevance

The data processing revolution has succeeded in swamping most organizations in data – but the relevance of much of the information produced is suspect. How relevant are the administrative functions to today's business needs? How relevant are the reports which are produced?

2.11.3 Accuracy

Accuracy for its own sake is a waste of money. A contentious statement maybe, but another analogy illustrates the point. What is the purpose of producing a payroll with calculations to 13 decimal places when currency only pays out to two decimal places? Many administrative services make broad assumptions and then build inverted pyramids of spurious accuracy on top of these assumptions. Perhaps the assumptions are based on best evidence but often they do not merit a level of accuracy which is then built around them. Indeed, this accuracy may actually mislead management in believing that the base assumption has a validity which it does not possess. Perhaps categories like 'high', 'medium', 'low' may be accurate enough. In any event, let us expose the base assumptions and not cloak them with the fallacious legitimacy of excess accuracy in subsequent processes. That way, the assumption itself can be questioned and better management decisions taken. The level of accuracy of output should therefore clearly reflect the level of accuracy of input or base assumptions.

2.11.4 Format

The format in which the administration delivers its services should be that which is most convenient to its customers. A tightly printed report consisting of columns of figures is less immediately meaningful than a graph or a pie chart. The format or packaging of the service should be negotiated with the customers.

2.11.5 Cost effectiveness

Many customers will simply not want a Rolls-Royce type service. Pursuit of excellence for its own sake can be expensive – cripplingly so. Despite the emphasis on quality standards – BS 5750 or ISO 9000 – the key issue on quality is that it should be appropriate, not that it should be ultimate. It is a truism that the cost of a service should not exceed its value – and yet many organizations do not balance cost against value, particularly the cost of administrative and support services. The SLA negotiations provide an environment in which this process can be objectively performed.

Many organizations have administrative functions simply because they have been there, unquestioned, over the years. Many administrative functions perform tasks simply because they have been doing them year upon year. We have all come across instances where reports are produced every month or every quarter and then these reports are filed, unseen. Yet more frequent are examples of individuals keying data from these reports into a personal computer to massage them into a spreadsheet or to produce graphics from them. If business analysis skills are brought to bear during the SLA negotiation it might be possible for the service to provide exactly what the customer needs more productively.

Schedules will be required for the administrative processes, together with instructions about the output from them. Quality control of the output – whether that is a canteen meal or a personnel record – may need to be included in the SLA. Escalation arrangements may need to made, to cover the timescale by which the customer should notify the service provider of delayed outputs.

In some cases delivery mechanisms should also be agreed for the SLA.

2.12 Remote services

Sometimes the service provider is remote from its customer. When considering the responsiveness of such service providers, the customer is concerned with the service they see from their location. It is responsiveness of the service at the customer's desks which is the key performance indicator, not the responsiveness within, say, corporation headquarters. There is little point in a head office legal service setting itself a two-day timescale in which to reply to queries if their reply sits in a messenger's tray for a fortnight thereafter.

Thus one of the main problems with remote services may be monitoring their availability and response through all of the communications channels to the customer's place of work. Initially it may be possible to measure the overall response through the various communication channels but, if service improvement and streamlining is to be achieved, it will be necessary to break down responsiveness into the various individual components that make up the communications change.

2.13 Subcontracts

The service provider is usually able to control the service elements for which they have direct line responsibility. However, issues arise when the service provider is reliant on others for part of the delivery of the service. This may either be because actual legal subcontracts are involved (for example, a maintenance contract for faulty equipment) or when logical subcontracts exist within an organization (for instance, reliance on an accounts department or information technology department). In this case responsibilities have to be clearly defined and handover points clearly established.

'Subcontractors' should be evaluated for:

- technical capability
- technical competence
- capacity
- past history
- test results against other suppliers

- experience of other customers
- financial viability.

2.14 Help desk and customer support

Many support functions have a help desk – either a formal structure or a *de facto* structure in which helpful individuals have been identified by customers. Customer satisfaction is usually increased by formalizing the help desk function to provide the customer with a clear point of contact. A help desk may be little more than a receptionist function, receiving calls and diverting them to the appropriate specialist, or it may be fully competent to resolve the majority of problems which it receives. It is highly unlikely, however, that the help desk will be able to provide a complete answer to **all** the queries it receives and inevitably some problems will be referred to specialists within the support area or possibly to external suppliers. Problem management procedures should be in place to ensure that 'ownership' of a problem is registered and that no problem can be 'un-owned'. 'Ownership' of a problem may either reside at the help desk regardless of where it is referred or 'ownership' may pass to the person to whom it is referred. In either case a problem manager should be appointed to review outstanding problems and to escalate them where necessary. The customer will be a party to deciding how to prioritize problems with the support service which they use. The customer may also help to set escalation procedure.

2.15 Security services

Since many of the customers will be reliant upon the support service being in place, they will be vulnerable in the event that it cannot be provided. A valid service offering is therefore a contingency arrangement to cover loss of service. Similarly standards may be required to protect the integrity of information of processes. Security services may therefore include:

- security reviews relating to the customer use of the support service
- management of equipment on behalf of the customer
- management of contractors or external suppliers on behalf of the customer
- provision of backup arrangements
- advice on legislation relating to the support area.

2.16 Special requirements

Where dedicated equipment, staff or facilities have been acquired for the customer or where non-standard support is provided, the service level requirement needs to be included in the SLA.

2.17 Standardization

Where a customer operates non-standard equipment or non-standard practices, support can be complex, time consuming and difficult to provide because the skill set required to support such customers can be very broad and high, and very complex. An SLA may therefore define standard equipment, practices or procedures which can be supported and service for non-standard items may be limited. Certain disciplines may be expected of the customer if they are to be properly supported – perhaps compliance with quality standards.

2.18 Customer self-help

Management fashions come and go, and we have seen an increasing emphasis on local autonomy and away from centralization in recent years. With this local autonomy, some internal customers will wish to take on an increasing part of the support role for themselves. In this case, handover standards and boundaries need to be clearly defined and formal acceptance from in-house supplier to customer may be advisable. Similarly, change management procedures may be required to ensure that changes introduced within the customer's area of responsibility do not impact adversely upon the service provider and vice versa.

2.19 Training

Customer requirements for training and the service provider's terms and conditions for providing it should be included in the SLA.

2.20 Customer satisfaction survey

The previous sections will help to define the scope of service and hours of service which the service supplier feels it should be providing. It should also unearth information about actual availability and performance. The next step is to add customer feedback to this so that the process of iteration can begin.

It is easy to get over-technical and to try to do too much with a customer satisfaction survey. It is therefore suggested that the customer satisfaction survey itself be kept to about four pages and avoid too much technical detail. It should aim to score the customer's perception of the quality of each service as it is delivered to them. It should also provide the customer perception of:

- availability
- responsiveness
- turnround
- ease of use
- documentation

- training
- what the hours of service should be
- acceptable outage of service
- cost or impact of service outage
- quality of help desk and customer support service.

Especially if this is the first time a customer satisfaction survey has been issued, this is probably about as much as one could expect a customer to complete by themselves.

Care should be taken with interpretation of the survey since folklore lingers – especially of poor service. In one case a customer cited 'bad' service and, when pressed, his example was of a service which had not been offered for several years.

Checklist 2, which follows at the end of this chapter, is intended to provoke thought on customer satisfaction and potential problem areas.

An example of a customer satisfaction survey follows Checklist 2. In subsequent chapters we will see how the more technical information can be drawn from the customer to supplement the customer satisfaction survey.

Checklist 2: Service level quantification – Critical component failure analysis

1. Quantify customer satisfaction with respect to:
   - access
   - availability
   - responsiveness
   - change management
   - support
   - problem-solving
   - services/products
   - cost.
2. Support functions – quantify:
   - 'noise level'
   - number of problems
     - resolved within target
     - unresolved
   - frequency of customer–supplier meetings
   - support service products and services (see also 5):
     - identify all services
     - identify cost of each
     - identify value of each
     - identify usage of each.
3. Service criticalities – quantify:
   - daily – critical periods
   - daily – prime time
   - end of month criticalities
   - end of week criticalities
   - end of year criticalities

- what are the critical times for each user?
- what is the value of the service at those times?
- what is the service quality of these critical times?
4. 'Ownership' – identify 'ownership' of and define responsibilities for:
    - equipment
    - services
      - who has priority?
    - channels of communications
    - distributed processes
    - consumables
    - databases
    - data
    - service changes
    - backup or security
    - problems associated with each of these.
5. For each service, examine critical components and communication paths to establish:
    - capacity/load:
      - present
      - forecast one year/three years
    - availability:
      - actual versus target
    - reliability:
      - of service elements
    - serviceability:
      - of component parts
      - mean time between failures (MTBF)
      - mean time to fix (MTTF)
    - performance:
      - response by type of job
    - supplied products and services:
      - what service offered?
      - from where?
      - on what equipment?
      - for whom?
      - when?

Sample customer satisfaction survey

Note

This survey is not intended to be exhaustive, but to serve as a prompt. Readers are invited to expand, delete, omit or include items to tailor it to their needs.

CUSTOMER SATISFACTION SURVEY

CUSTOMER DETAILS

Initials:

Surname:

Reference:

Telephone No.:

Date:

CUSTOMER ACCOUNT MANAGER DETAILS

Name:

Address:

Telephone No.:

1. **Please rate your services on a scale of 1 (poor) to 6 (excellent).** (Use a separate form for each service product.)

   Service product:———————————

Service availability
Response time
Turnround time
Ease of use
Help facilities
Documentation
News and service information
Customer training

   Please use this space if you wish to enlarge on any of your above responses:

2. **Please specify below which service product is the highest priority and the impact to you of a loss of service.**

Product/service	*Service hours*	*Maximum acceptable delay*	*Cost/impact of delay*
	Monday–Friday:	Normal:	Normal:
	'Normal working day'	Critical periods:	Critical periods:
	'Extended working day'		
	Other times:		

Critical periods are:_____

3. **Please rate the following functions of the help desk and customer care service on a scale of 1 (poor) to 6 (excellent). Please leave blank if not known or not applicable**

First level help desk
Availability of support staff
Access to specialist staff
Help with problem-solving
Promptness of response to queries
Effectiveness of response to queries
Staff friendliness

Please use this space if you wish to enlarge on any of your above responses:

4. **Development, design and creative services: please rate your experiences with development on a scale of 1 (poor) to 6 (excellent).**

Consultancy skills

Business analysis skills

Capture of requirement

Creative capabilities

Design skills

Project management skills

Delivery to time

Delivery to budget

Handover as operational

Effectiveness of what was delivered

Defect rate

Defect correction

Handling of new requirements/enhancements

Friendliness/cooperation of service staff

Service orientation of service staff

5. **Delivery mechanism: please rate your experiences with development on a scale of 1 (poor) to 6 (excellent).**

Availability

Defect rate

Defect correction

Voice (telephone)

Fax services

Telex services

Transport services

Courier services

Handling of new requests

Maintenance (if appropriate)

Friendliness/cooperation of service staff

Technical skill of service staff

Service orientation of service staff

6. **Other services (refers to any other services, not previously specified, which the customer may receive):**

7. **Please specify any new service products you feel would improve the service already provided:**

Would you be prepared to contribute to any additional costs involved?

Yes ☐ No ☐

8. **Additional comments:**

3

How service level agreements apply in a development or creative environment

3.1 Creative and development functions

SLAs are normally thought of as applying to an ongoing production service. Conceptually it is more difficult to imagine them in the volatile development and creative processes. However, production SLAs can be made more effective – and service provided more cost-effectively and to a higher quality – if the SLA concept is embraced during concept or development stages.

Today there is growing pressure for development services and for creative functions to be clearly oriented to business solutions and to deliver quickly and cheaply. These characteristics tend to militate against service level criteria being specified at the design stages of the development project or the concept stages of a creative project and being checked as such projects progress. The development and creative functions can result in a very high end cost. Because market conditions are so uncertain, customer taste fickle and fashions transient it may be advisable to limit risk by market research, piloting or prototyping. To reduce downside risk and to avoid runaway costs, there is pressure to deliver development projects in stages and creative work in modules.

But availability, usability, throughput and other service level issues are crucial to the success of any development or creative project.

The price for ignoring service level aspects may be high:

- up to nine out of ten service-related businesses fail within the first five years of their life;
- 'runaway projects' cost the UK over £500 million a year;
- many advertising campaigns have produced memorable advertisements – which backfired because the creative content swamped the product message.

Poor service level achievement may not be the only reason for these failures – but it is a significant contributing factor in many of them. How can we avoid similar mistakes? Definition of the service objectives is one key criteria. There is no reason why solid service criteria cannot be established for creative services. Criteria may be:

- the television commercial should be capable of a three-year life without being obviously outdated;
- the effectiveness of an advertising campaign should be measurable in increased sales of $x\%$ within a six-month period;
- an advertising campaign should be capable of increasing market share by $x\%$ within a twelve month period;
- after the advertising campaign, market research should indicate customer awareness of the product has increased by $x\%$.

Quality is another key factor. If quality is built into the development or creative process from concept on through to delivery, not only will the result be more effective, it will be more robust and more serviceable.

Defects in production services are a prime cause of service unavailability. Even if they do not make the service unavailable, they can make it unusable or make it impossible to support a good service. Various surveys show that it can cost over 100 times more to correct a defect in a production environment than it costs to eliminate it at the design stage.

We can also draw an analogy with computer systems analysts. Even a good computer systems analyst is likely to capture only 60% of the requirement. The inevitable communication gap between analyst and customer contributes to this. Within any creative or development environment, a similar communication gap can exist. The clear and unambiguous specification of the objectives from a development or creative process is therefore of prime importance.

Quality has a payback: after implementing quality methods, IBM saved over $2 billion on defect correction in a three-year period. These are big numbers, but proportionate savings are possible on any service. That is one reason why service level management frequently forms an integral part of quality programmes.

We have seen earlier that service management methodologies have to be in place before an SLA can be applied to production services. In exactly the same way, formal development methodologies or methodologies for control of creative processes have to be in place before we can commit ourselves to an SLA in those environments – and realistically, before we can deliver a given level of service to the results of those processes. Service level requirements should be an integral part of the specification in the development and creative processes and acceptance of the results of such processes should depend on meeting service level criteria.

The key approaches required are summarized in Figure 3.1 and in the following sections.

3.2 Standards

There should be a corporate overall framework of standards within which the development or creative processes take place. Overall standards should be set and

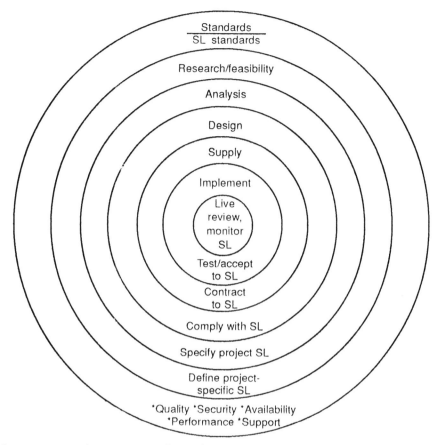

Figure 3.1   Development or creative environment.

development or creative functions should be motivated to comply with these standards.

3.3 Feasibility study

A feasibility study needs to assist in the definition of basic service criteria relevant to the proposed new development or creative process. These will be defined as the process progresses. For ease of reference, the product or service resulting from the development or creative process is referred to as 'the output'. It should involve:

- establishing basic definition of project-specific service levels
- establishing downside risks of failure to complete project
- considering performance issues:
  - response
  - turnround
  - efficiency (in terms of capacity requirement)
- considering freshness or longevity of the result (what is its life?)

- considering total life of the output relative to the business requirement (what do we do after its death?)
- considering support requirements
- budgeting for ongoing support costs
- budgeting for project management costs
- budgeting for quality assurance/quality control
- budgeting for security
- including risk analysis
- assessing value of the output arising from the development or creative process
- assessing impact of loss of the output once the development or creative process is complete.

3.4 Analysis/specification

The analysis and specification stage needs to include:

- a structured approach to analysis
- establishing reliability service level (defining frequency/nature of errors permissible)
- establishing availability service level
- establishing throughput service level
- specifying freshness (otherwise currency – how up-to-date is the output required to be?)
- specifying minimum life of the output
- specifying formats required for the output
- setting response service level
- accurate sizing and capacity planning to provide a robust growth plan in line with (or over) forecast growth over the life of the output
- quality control
- quality assurance
- security
- fault tolerance.

3.5 Design

Design functions should include:

- the service specification processes
- quality of bought-in products and services
- quality control or service level of the service in design and operation
- implementing design reviews at each development phase
- validating service delivery is in line with the service specifications
- managing change during development.

    The design stage needs to include:

- structured approach to design

- design for usability
- design for output longevity
- quality assurance
- compliance with service levels specified in terms of:
  - impact
  - effectiveness
  - availability
  - throughput
  - response
  - turnround
  - longevity
  - usability
  - sizing/capacity
  - flexibility
  - security
- quality control
- accurate and comprehensive documentation.

3.6 Invitation to tender/contract

The development or creative process may result in a requirement to buy in additional equipment or services. The evaluation and acquisition processes and contractual stages should reflect the service level requirement previously defined. In particular, they should:

- include service level requirements as part of the invitation to tender;
- include service level requirements as part of the contractual requirements;
- provide for a clause in the contract for retention of a significant part of the payment after delivery until acceptance testing (including performance to service level standards) has been completed;
- include penalty clauses for non-compliance with service level requirements
- specify training requirement
- specify documentation requirements
- specify support requirements:
  - maintenance (cover and response)
  - help desks/other support
  - output life over which support is required
- investigate financial status of supplier and ultimate vendor to be assured of their viability over the life of the output (where ongoing maintenance or support is needed).

3.7 Implementation

At implementation stage, from a service level viewpoint the key activity is testing to ensure the delivered system meets service level requirements. Acceptance testing may therefore include:

- volume testing (peak volumes and forecast volumes)
- permutation testing (all possible permutations of demand on the service)
- performance testing (to service level specifications)
- effectiveness or usability testing:
  - by service provider
  - by ultimate customer or end-user
- sign-off from development or creative team and acceptance into production
- sign-off and acceptance by customer.

3.8 Post-implementation review

The post-implementation review should include:

- performance against service level specification
- current utilization against forecast sizing
- anticipated growth against original forecast growth
- current impact of loss of service against that identified at feasibility study and design stages
- documentation in use compared with specification
- adequacy of training.

3.9 Service orientation

Customers may be more likely to assume service level requirements than to specify them: it is the supplying department's role to ensure that all requirements are covered in the specification and to ensure they are met before delivery of the output.

4

Keys to measuring and monitoring service: designing and implementing an SLA

4.1 Measuring performance and availability

How do we get objective information about performance and availability?

One starting point for service monitoring could be the resource monitoring facilities on equipment used by the service provider. Most computers, and many peripheral devices, electro-mechanical and mechanical equipment generate information about resource utilization and performance. In addition, computer software may produce further performance information. Telephone exchanges may also contain information on volumes, throughput and availability (in terms of calls getting the 'engaged' tone). Network monitors too may provide performance and availability information. An on-line computer application could perform some of its own response time monitoring by having the transaction time-stamped on its journey from the terminal, through the network nodes into the host and back to the terminal. This information could then be piggy-backed onto the next transaction and extracted for analysis at the host.

Incident and problem management procedures may identify service outages and their duration. The help desk may record problem information which also reflects downtime or service outage. Engineers' logs may contain yet more data on performance. Where there is a capacity planning function, it needs to establish utilization and performance in order to make sensible decisions about equipment sizing for the future: this data is again of value for service level management.

Performance and availability data may therefore be spread over a very wide area, involving different people perhaps from different departments within the organization. Bringing all this information together may not only make for more efficiency by avoiding duplication of effort but it can provide the basis of a service management database. There are a number of software tools available which can be used to consolidate information from resource monitors into a database. By adding information from incident and problem reporting systems and from manual logs this database may be enhanced and possibly could become the single focal point for management of the service.

From this service database we could draw historic information which will greatly assist in critical component failure analysis.

Since the service database may also contain utilization information it can underpin an equitable policy for charging for our services.

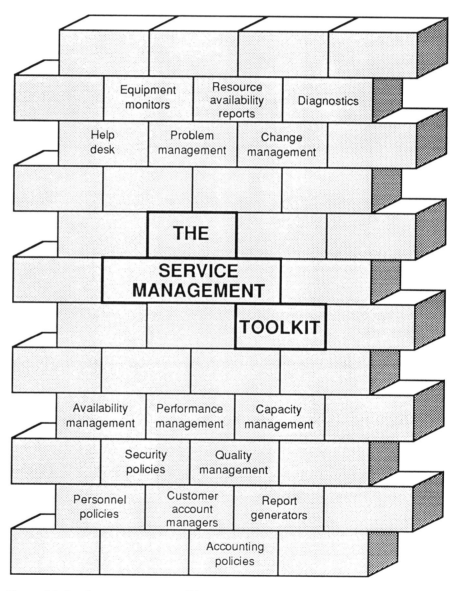

Figure 4.1 Service management toolkit.

Trend information from the service database will help to identify areas where availability and performance are declining: if regular trend reports are produced the 'hot spots' are quickly revealed.

Monitoring of activity between different locations is frequently more problematical. Monitoring can suffer from a number of disadvantages:

- lack of standardization of downstream information
- inconsistency between different manufacturers, or suppliers, or sites, in definition and presentation of faults
- difficulty (or impossibility) in identifying or cross referring a fault reported simultaneously by different customers
- failure of the service management systems if equipment on which they operate fails
- imposition of a significant overhead on the service provider by the monitoring processes
- difficulty in central monitoring of downstream components, the failure of which may impact on service levels.

The aim, however, should be to develop a cost effective monitoring capability which:

- tracks the number of defects as they arise, enabling rectification sometimes even before customers notice the problem;
- shows average response for service components monitored;
- monitors all generic service products showing monthly response time trends;
- monitors individual service products against the number of transactions:
  - shows peak hour and average daily customer utilization;
  - operates by identifying responsiveness 'at the customer's desk' or 'in the customer's hands'.

Such a capability does not, however, come cheap. One alternative to the monitoring methods described above is to monitor performance 'at the desk' by introducing a periodic test basket of transactions and recording response time for later analysis. This approach was taken by IBM when implementing their National Office Support System (NOSS).

Whatever monitoring method is used, the service quality has to be measurable, and the measurements have to be demonstrably objective to the customer.

Chapter 2 identified the importance of having service management disciplines in place before embarking on SLAs. The diagnostic and monitoring tools above add to the service management toolkit (see Figure 4.1) with which we can start to build an SLA.

4.2 Balancing detail with practicality

It is easy to get hooked on the measurement processes. It is tempting to measure everything that is measurable and to include all of it in an SLA. That is not necessarily what the customer wants.

We have seen how quantification and measurement can help in the context of critical component failure analysis. This level of detail is of considerable value to the service provider internally – to help to introduce alternative paths to improve service resilience, to identify where and how to build resilience into operational processes and delivery mechanisms, and to help create the business justification for the cost of this resilience. But most of this detailed information is probably not of particular importance to the customer. Too much detail can be indigestible.

Appendix A is an SLA checklist, developed from one produced by George W. Miller for use by American Airlines. It is a lengthy checklist, but the pages consist only of headings! The headings cover most of the items which one could consider (but not necessarily include) when designing an SLA. While all the topics in the checklist should be considered, only the key items should be selected for use in a pilot SLA. If one were to include all those headings, the final SLA could run into several volumes!

4.3 What to include in an SLA

Especially when embarking on implementation of an SLA for the first time, this checklist approach has much to recommend it. It will ensure key items will not be overlooked, and it enforces a consistent approach across different customers. Following the checklist tends to force decisions on what should and should not be included in an SLA and it greatly assists the education process (for both support service staff and customers).

Broadly, an SLA should cover the following topics:

- purpose of SLA
- duration of agreement
- description of service:
  - service overview
  - corporate dependence
  - priority
  - critical periods
  - peak periods
  - impact and cost of outage
  - availability:
    - definition of availability
    - availability targets (which may be for the service as a whole, or for each component of the service)
  - transaction throughput and arrival rates (number of similar items handled or jobs done):
    - standard day
    - peak periods
  - response requirements (the time it should take to handle an item or complete job):
    - for each transaction type
    - definition of response
  - forecast utilization and growth/decline:
    - now
    - projected growth in six months

             projected growth in one year
             projected growth in two years
- background work details (i.e. routine tasks which can be scheduled as opposed to real-time work to be completed immediately it is presented):
             deadlines for input to the service provider
             turnround targets
             output arrangements
- ancillary requirements
- accuracy:
             of input
             of production processes
             of output
- security:
             of input
             of production processes
             of output
             backup
             disaster recovery and contingency planning
- service hours
- scheduled unavailability:
  - for maintenance
  - for changes
  - bank and public holidays
- support hours:
  - help desk
  - technical or professional support
  - customer account management arrangements
- problem escalation procedure
- charging arrangements (if applicable)
- change control
- service level measurement
- monitoring actual service level against SLA targets
- service level reporting
- penalties for failure
- arrangements for customer service review meetings
- contacts
- duration of agreement and renegotiation arrangements.

Appendices could deal with detail about charging algorithms, scheduling and discount arrangements and definitions. Details of standard services or standard tariffs could also be included as appendices.

4.4 Shell, template, model and standard SLAs

There are many ways of designing an SLA:

4.4.1 Shell SLA

A shell SLA is a standard format with a series of headings – like the checklist at Appendix A. The assumption in using a shell SLA is that each customer's needs are likely to be unique. Inconsistencies between SLAs can arise from different interpretations of the shell checklist.

4.4.2 Template SLA

A template SLA covers every service type, all service levels and all customer types. It would never be implemented as it stands: much of it would be irrelevant to any specific customer. Its value lies in being the comprehensive SLA encyclopaedia from which just the relevant clauses can be drawn for an SLA for any single customer or service.

4.4.3 Model SLA

A model SLA is intended to be an equitable framework within which the terms will be negotiated for each customer. A model SLA represents the normal conditions of providing service but expects these to be modified in practice.

4.4.4 Standard SLA

A standard SLA is often applied by commercial service companies and is often more of a contractual document. It specifies terms and conditions which would not normally be varied. A standard SLA may be vague on specific performance criteria and heavy on reasons for non-fulfilment of targets since it frequently favours the service vendor over the customer.

While each type of SLA has its benefits, for an in-house service, the model SLA will probably be favoured.

4.5 The service handbook

A service handbook could simplify and supplement SLAs by removing detail – especially transient detail – from the SLA (transient detail refers to any short life information, such as information about equipment used, schedules which may be temporary and names and telephone numbers where these may change). The service handbook could contain:

- service mission statement
- overview of the service
- equipment used to provide the service

- standard dependencies
- standards required of customers
- standard service menu
- standard terms and conditions
- default of standard service levels
- standard security arrangements and security advice
- standard contingency planning arrangements
- standard problem management arrangements (e.g. help desk and escalation procedures)
- technical or professional support details
- standard scheduled service outages
- charging:
  - standard tariff rates
  - charging algorithms
  - accounting reports
- menu of 'gold star' options (premium services)
- menu of special services (bespoke services)
- service provider's contacts (names and details).

4.6 Service level survey

There was deliberately no technical detail in the customer satisfaction survey discussed earlier. Whereas the customer satisfaction survey can be completed by the customer without assistance from the service provider, the specification of a service level in technical terms will probably be a process of exploration and explanation between a customer and a representative of the service provider, translating business terms (the terminology used by the service receiver, e.g. the production of invoices, debits, journal entries, etc.) into technical terminology (the terms used by the service provider, e.g. quantities of materials or consumables used, and detailed specifications, e.g. weight of paper, water pressure, temperature, megabytes of storage, band rates, definition of 'transaction', etc.).

A service level survey can standardize and formalize this process. If this is completed by a representative from the service provider in discussion with the customer, and jointly agreed, it can be signed off by both and can form the basis of the SLA. More text and details can then be added.

Many of the components of service level management will be in place (see Figure 4.2).

4.7 Charging for services

As we have just seen service providers tend to judge their achievements in terms of their own professional speciality and terminology. Thus an accounting function may think in terms of payments made, a personnel function in terms of staff reports or recruitment interviews. However, the view that the business customers have of the service is often far less detailed and attaches emphasis to different aspects. The

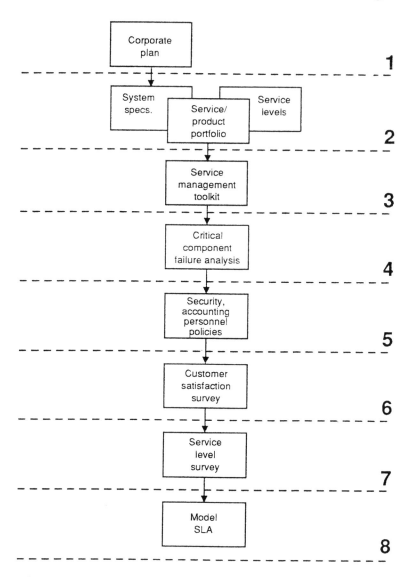

Figure 4.2 Components of service level management.

marketing function is likely to judge the accounts department on its ability to deliver sales reports by area and sales person, preferably on demand but certainly within, say, three working days of the end of the accounting period. An employing department is likely to judge the personnel function on the promptness of filling vacancies with new employees of appropriate calibre and the speed at which it handles promotions and pay changes. But these are just some of the service products provided by the respective support services.

How, objectively, can we measure a support service except in terms of what it costs, what it saves and what it earns? Unless a support service is required by legislation (perhaps health and safety), only the users of the service can say whether the spend on it is worthwhile. The solution is often therefore seen as to charge the users for internal services and let them vote with their budgets whether or not to use them.

There are snags with the charging approach:

- Charging may just result in under-utilization of corporate assets which have already been paid for.
- There has to be a critical mass of customers for a service to be cost-effective. It may cost little more to run a heavily utilized service than it does to run a lightly loaded service.
- Unless there is strong central control, charging may merely duplicate spend on the service as users buy their own equipment (or buy in external commercial services) which they perceive to be cheaper than using the corporate support service.
- Job accounting systems cost money: they are a processing overhead and cost in staff time of the service supplier – this cost will ultimately be passed back to the customers of the service.

But it may be thought that if SLAs are to be meaningful, the cost of the service should be charged out. So, despite these snags, the decision may be to proceed with charging. If so, a mechanism has to be found to convert resource utilization into cash cost.

There are several possible approaches:

- cost notification
- cost allocation
- charge-out.

4.7.1 Cost notification

With cost notification, usually the cost of running the service is established and its users are advised of the amount that is attributable to their use. This is toothless: real charges are not applied and a typical reaction is a shrug and the comment 'so what?' However, cost notification is sometimes seen as the first step towards cost allocation or charge-out to give the wasteful customer due warning to become more efficient in the use of the service's resources (and to force economies on the service provider) before real bills are imposed.

4.7.2 Cost allocation

Cost allocation identifies the total cost of the service and allocates it, usually according to usage, to customers of the service. Since the customers may have had little opportunity to establish whether the cost is reasonable, cost allocation is often viewed as an inescapable and unjust tax imposed by the unaccountable. Cost allocation frequently causes a sense of grievance against the service providers. Its customers may argue that the service provider can spend what it likes – but it is the customer who picks up the bill for it. But if cost allocation is an interim step to charge-out, the writing is on the wall for the profligate service provider.

4.7.3 Charge-out

A charge-out system bills the customers with the actual costs they incur – and may be accompanied by the right for internal customers to go to alternative sources of supply for the service. If so, the service provider may be allowed to tout for external work – perhaps on the way to becoming a fully commercial bureau business. The main issues in a charge-out system are the charge-out units and their price.

At the same time, cost recovery policies have to be set. Most customers would object to a strictly demand-based **break even** recovery policy, where the price of a job could vary according to utilization of the service. On a lightly loaded service the cost of a job this week could be more than the same job would cost the next week, when the service was more heavily loaded with more customers or higher throughput to share or spread the cost. Such a policy penalizes the loyal, regular users and complicates their budgetary planning. It should, however, recover exactly the cost of the service. In practice, the cost of the service is usually taken over an accounting period or financial year to smooth out the variations.

A **standard** costing system would establish the average utilization, create a unit of charge, and base the price of that unit on the average utilization. However, while a breakeven policy should result in balanced books for the service supplier, a standard costing policy could result in either a profit or a loss depending on whether the forecast average utilization was under-achieved, correct, or over-achieved.

The next issue is to establish the mechanism for calculating the costs of each service product. Most pieces of equipment and some software will have integral counters or software to record the usage made of them. Thus computer usage, pages of print, number of microfiches, etc., can be identified by each type of service job. Human resource time recording systems or job accounting systems may also have (human) resource monitoring capabilities.

The utilization of these resources can be identified and from this a representative composite resource unit (RU) can be created. An RU is thus an average of resources used. By examining various types of job, or various transactions, we can identify how many RUs each one takes. This then gives us another average cost, expressed in RUs, for each type of job or transaction.

This average cost in RUs can be described as a workload unit (WU). We can now express the cost of providing the support service in terms of WUs. As far as the customers of the service go, the RU and WU are of no interest. The customers are interested in how much it costs to recruit a member of staff, to issue a cheque, or to make a payroll payment. So the next step is to translate the cost of these customer business activities in terms of business workload units (BWUs). From this we can put a cash cost on each customer business activity: we can now say what each insurance policy, meal or delivery costs in cash terms based on the equipment involved.

WUs have identified equipment (and possibly software) resources per job. General support costs may also be included – maintenance, depreciation, people costs and other items. Support costs specific to a customer may be charged out directly. This charging method is illustrated in Figure 4.3.

We can vary costs to encourage utilization smoothing – like the telecommunications companies which charge higher tariffs at certain peak times of day and cheaper tariffs at off-peak times. We could go so far at to create different charging regimes to

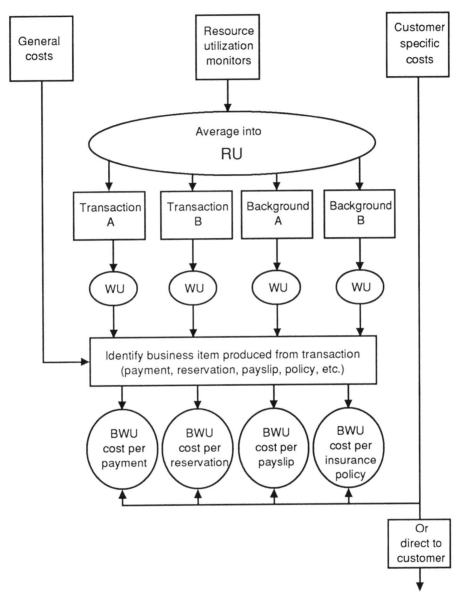

Figure 4.3 Charging for support services – schematic.

smooth the workload peak into a manageable mound – and so, perhaps, defer expensive equipment, purchases or recruitment of additional staff. We could offer an 'express' service – but at a higher cost. Charging therefore offers considerable scope as a service capacity management tool – but only if the user is made to become committed to using the service for a reasonable length of time.

What, then, is a reasonable length of time? That partly depends on the service provider's proportion of fixed to non-fixed costs and the amount of investment in capital equipment. Depending on its nature, equipment may be written off over anything from twelve months to ten years. The user commitment to the service should bear a reasonable relationship to the write-off period of any equipment involved. Whereas a heavy plant may not depreciate rapidly (say a ten year write-off) electronic equipment may rapidly lose its value and be written off over a period of, say, three years. What that means is that the service provider may be saddled with heavy depreciation costs and heavy running costs for the write-off life of the equipment. These represent high, effectively fixed, costs which can be undercut by competitor service as soon as a new model or an equipment price reduction is announced. The service provider therefore has one of three choices:

- to maintain the WU price at broadly the same real cost (allowing for inflation) over the life of the equipment, while competitive costs may be dropping;
- to drop the price for each WU in line with market forces and to seek operational economies to prevent under-recovery of costs;
- to inflate the price for each WU in the early years of the equipment when external competition is less and reduce costs in line with market forces later.

From the service provider's viewpoint, the ideal is to commit the customer to use the service for the life of the equipment, at a price which will recover capital and operational costs and which will remain broadly in line with competitor services over the life of the equipment.

Unfortunately, the service provider may not be able to determine its own charging policy; frequently this is decided upon by corporate accountants who will not allow over-recovery in the early years to offset future under-recovery as competition strengthens and usage patterns change.

4.8 Infinite capacity and 100% availability?

It was stated earlier that customers are increasingly expecting a utility service, with the support service available whenever they want it with whatever capacity they require. The SLA can be the vehicle whereby a cost-benefit analysis is undertaken on a customer-by-customer, service-by-service basis to establish a balance between cost, availability and capacity that enables corporate targets to be met in the most cost-effective way.

4.8.1 Capacity cornucopia

Parkinson's Law can apply to service capacity, too: given an excess of capacity, customers' usage may expand to fill it (or the service provider will expand the job to fill the capacity!).

The SLA can be used to discourage use of resources. Complex enquiries or reports might, perhaps, be given a lower priority or scheduled into a non-prime regime. Exceptional authority could be required to increase the priority or change the regime.

Similarly there might be a standard default time during which a manned service may be available and after which an answerphone or voice response system only might be provided. The SLA negotiations could explore these possibilities with customers.

If the service is charged out the SLA can include standard costs for standard jobs and a higher tariff for non-standard jobs. Equally, the charging policy could encourage the transfer of work from one type of service to another.

4.8.2 Absolute availability

Does your organization really need 100% service availability? Does it appreciate the price this involves? After all, 99.8% availability is relatively easy to achieve these days, and although 99.9% is trickier, it is not impossible. After that it gets harder and costs exponentially more. It cost Bell around 1000 man years of effort to improve the availability of computerized telephone switching systems from 99.9% to 99.98% – let alone the hardware cost. For many organizations, the spend to achieve a marginal improvement in availability may simply not be cost justified. We get into the laws of diminishing returns. But to another organization, 100% availability of the support service – say high-value engineering maintenance – may represent the competitive edge that will enable them to capture crucial market share.

The same is true of technical and professional support – especially people. If support is allowed to be entirely demand driven, either the same people get increasingly stretched – with consequent frustration and increase in staff turnover – or more staff are recruited and costs escalate. If charging is applied, support outside standard hours could rate a 'gold star' (more expensive) tariff.

The SLA process should help to establish the justifiable level of availability for each application or service.

4.9 Realistic limits to service

We have seen how SLAs can help to establish the realistic limits to service in terms of availability, capacity and performance. Other limits to service may be:

- territorial:
  - to define where the customer's 'territory' starts
  - to exclude remote equipment
  - to exclude locations where high security requirements or poor physical or telecommunications access inhibits service provision
  - to exclude locations which the service provider's resources are unable to support
- service:
  - to exclude services beyond the skills or capability of the service provider to support
- technological:
  - to define 'the equipment', 'the system' or 'the technology' on which the services are offered
  - to encourage standardization
  - to exclude certain types of equipment

- to exclude certain software
- to exclude or limit responsibilities for activities undertaken by third parties
- to exclude certain hi-tech high-risk activities
- logistical:
  - to allow for scheduled service outages
  - to take account of unscheduled outages
  - to take account of physical difficulties
- quality:
  - to deny or limit service to customers who fail to apply adequate quality assurance or quality control
  - to deny or limit service for service products which have not been developed or tested to quality standards
- financial:
  - to limit the degree of financial exposure to a single customer
  - to place a lower limit of spend on a customer
- security:
  - to deny or limit service or access in the interests of security
  - to exclude high-risk areas (vulnerable to fraud or other security breach)
- functional:
  - to define each party's responsibilities
- contingent:
  - upon the customer fulfilling certain obligations, typically:
    compliance with input delivery deadlines
    compliance with accuracy requirements
    compliance with volume or utilization forecasts
    compliance with minimum or maximum spend
  - upon suppliers delivering service:
    internal suppliers
    external suppliers
  - upon resources (staff, tools or equipment) being available.

4.10 Procurement

Many a service provider has been accused of being an ivory tower, but (to mix the metaphors) no service provider is an island. It can only deliver service if services are delivered to it by a number of other suppliers. In committing itself to SLAs, the service provider needs to tie its suppliers to deliver their services that will enable the SLAs to be met. Figure 4.4 illustrates the need for back-to-back SLAs with both internal and external suppliers.

Bought-in products or services may be critical in delivering the service to the SLA requirements. It may be necessary to have SLAs with suppliers, or to include performance specifications in contracts. In any event, it is recommended that procurement be made to defined international or national standards and that ISO 9001, ISO 9002 or ISO 9003, as appropriate, be used when buying products or services.

Procurement should include:

- purchase orders with specifications

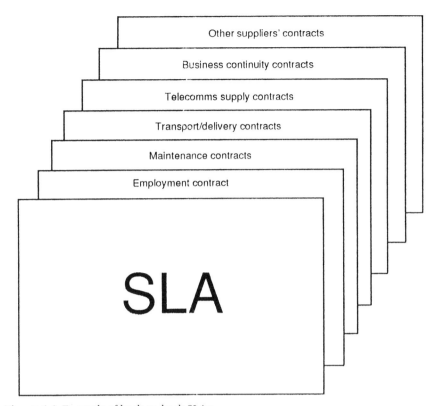

Figure 4.4 Example of back-to-back SLAs.

- evaluation of subcontractors or sub-suppliers
- specification of quality requirements
- provision for arbitration in the event of disputes
- controls over increasing goods or services
- quality records for incoming goods or services.

4.11 Organizational issues

We have seen power shift from the service supplier to the customer. The consequent trend has been to treat all users as customers who pay for the service used. The service organization needs to reflect this: the organization should help to establish or reinforce the new service orientation. Merely implementing SLAs and establishing a help desk or 'customer support' function helps, but is not enough. Full service culture needs to be adopted.

The culture change works best if welcomed and supported from the top and pushed from below – with support from the customer. Figure 4.5 shows a model hierarchy for SLA implementation, in which the **sponsors** establish policy and create impetus for SLAs, **executants** are involved in negotiation and implementation of them, and **monitors** ensure compliance with them and report on divergence between the service agreed and delivered.

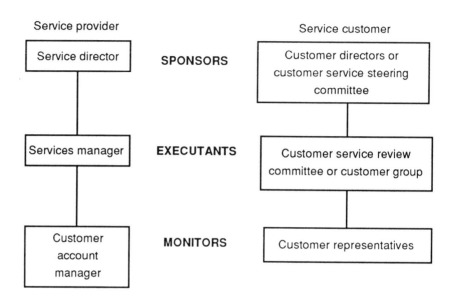

Figure 4.5 Hierarchy for SLA implementation.

4.11.1 Customer account managers

Customer account managers may be nominated for each major customer of the service. This may not necessarily be a full-time role: in a medium-sized organization or one with relatively few major customers or services, existing staffing may be nominated to exercise a secondary customer account management function. In a bigger or more complex service organization the customer account management function could be included as part of the responsibilities of several existing management or customer care roles.

Whether the service operates a genuine bureau operation with external commercial customers, or whether it is an in-house service, the role of the customer account manager will be to manage customer accounts to ensure the services provided meet customer needs, and to optimize the customer's use of the service. While the help desk or service desk remains the focal point for customer problems, the customer account manager will be the focal point for the customer to raise general service issues, for monitoring of performance against SLAs and for identifying new opportunities – essentially for marketing the service to that customer.

The customer account manager will also be responsible for coordinating all the service provider's activities necessary to meet the SLA or an agreed customer requirement. Liaison within the service provider's organization is a key part of the job: it involves taking full responsibility for delivery of service to the customer – and sorting out any internal problems, procedures or political in-fighting necessary. This means there is, internally, a large number of functions and individuals with whom the customer account manager needs to establish – and maintain – contact. A schematic of the liaison points is given in Figure 4.6.

Figure 4.6 Customer account manager: liaison points.

4.11.2 A marketing-oriented approach

Especially where customers are charged and are given the right to find alternative sources of supply of services, it may be worth taking this philosophy a stage further – to a full marketing-oriented approach. If the service provider has to be competitive to survive, it needs to equip itself with marketing skills: the appointment of a marketing and sales manager may be a natural corollary.

Example terms of reference for marketing and sales managers and for customer account managers follow this chapter.

4.11.3 Preparing the ground

Success in implementing SLAs is less likely if they are just launched on an unsuspecting customer. The ground needs to be prepared first. The ECRIT methodology is designed to address the fundamental marketing, resource and management prerequisites. ECRIT is an acronym derived from **E**duction, **C**ommitment, **R**esources, **I**nfrastructure and **T**actics). The ECRIT model for preparation will include the following:

4.11.4 Education

The education of:

- management
- the service provider's staff
- customers

by:

- raising the topic at customer meetings
- circulating internal papers on SLAs, highlighting benefits
- circulating copies of articles on SLAs from journals and magazines
- writing articles on SLAs for in-house newsletters
- preparing presentations for:
  - senior management
  - the service provider's management and staff
  - customers
- preparing handouts containing:
  - reasons for introducing SLAs
  - identification of benefits
  - sample SLA
  - sample reports
  - proposals for implementation, monitoring and review.

4.11.5 Commitment

Commitment to the service culture is essential from:

- general management
- the service provider's management and staff
- customers
- suppliers.

4.11.6 Resources

Resources need to be made available in terms of:

- budget
- staff
- equipment and tools.

4.11.7 Infrastructure

The infrastructure for SLAs needs to include:

- service management methodologies
- measurement tools
- monitoring and reporting tools.

4.11.8 Tactics

SLAs don't just happen, they have to be implemented to a potential tactical plan. The tactical plan could include, for implementation, use of a pilot SLA for a particular service or a particular customer (rather than trying to tackle all services for all customers at once); it also needs to include a monitoring and review process. SLAs can be expected as normal practice for new customers and/or new services. ECRIT is an acronym (mentioned earlier) - the pun is merely intended to emphasize that, once SLAs are presented as normal practice, this is unlikely to be challenged especially by new customers or for new services.

4.12 Pilot implementation

Before implementing an SLA generally it is well worthwhile trying it out on one specific pilot group. What are the characteristics of an appropriate victim?

The pilot customer should be selected to provide a range and depth of experience of implementing the servicing of an SLA. It should contain:

- a fairly large number of individual users
- a dominant service
- reasonable variety, e.g. a number of different delivery mechanisms or sites
- a quality of service requirement
- preferably a single point of contact with the service provider
- a reasonable relationship with the service provider
- commitment
- a good chance of success!

It is probably also helpful if the major activity of the members of the pilot group requires either the same service product or a family of service products that forms a coherent whole.

It may be possible to test the water with the customer by broaching the subject of SLAs informally or at any existing regular service review meetings. Any informal discussion on the principles of SLAs can lead to an agreement in principle to explore the possibilities.

We can use the checklists and outline SLAs previously discussed to quantify the service requirements of the pilot group and the existing level of service to them.

If we have had to troubleshoot for this group in the past we may already be familiar with some of their requirements.

A customer account manager can be nominated for them. Success or failure of this pilot may determine whether SLAs are implemented throughout the organization: the choice of customer account manager is therefore of vital importance. Tact and interpersonal skills are probably more important than technical or professional skills so the customer account manager for the pilot group might be more senior than would be the case in an ongoing situation.

The SLA hierarchy (see Figure 4.5) can be followed to underline and reinforce commitment from both the service provider and the customer.

A pilot exercise should probably last for between three and six months: it may well take six months to implement and see the results of any changes to the service quality. It should be made clear at the outset that there are likely to be changes in either the service or the service level agreement or both during the pilot period: to avoid later embarrassment the SLA should be treated as a draft in that period and not cast in stone.

At the end of the pilot period either the service or the SLA will be adjusted in the light of experience gained. Monitoring tools and methods and reporting formats may also undergo change.

4.13 Negotiating with the customer

The customer's initial response to the concept of SLAs may well be: 'At last I'm going to be able to tie down the service provider to actually deliver.' This initial enthusiasm may fade as the customer realizes that the negotiation is a two-way process and that they, the customer, are going to have to commit themselves to a certain level of usage, to meet input deadlines and accuracy objectives and all those other targets which are prerequisites for the service provider to achieve the service levels the customer wishes to establish.

In general, the customer is primarily interested in:

- cost (if the service is charged out)
- availability (only when they need it, but all the time they need it)
- performance (chiefly response)
- accessibility (access to the service should be quick and easy – for instance without complex ordering or booking procedures)
- output delivery
- problem-solving and escalation
- security (but only when things go wrong!)
- monitoring of performance against the SLA.

The negotiation process can only work effectively if these concerns are acknowledged. Negotiations are more likely to be effective if they are conducted in language the customer understands, with a high degree of openness and in a non-adversarial style designed to create a 'win-win' situation. For a commercial customer, a bureau is likely to want to protect itself by setting less stringent service targets than an in-house service might set for in-house customers since in the latter case their joint aim should be to serve the interests of their business as a whole.

Because resources are finite, it may be difficult, if not impossible, to guarantee a service to a single customer without taking account of the needs of all customers: the negotiation needs to get this point across. The opportunity can also be taken to set realistic expectations of the pilot SLAs and to identify a fairly short timescale for SLA review.

The length of time it takes to negotiate an SLA should not be underestimated. If a template, standard or model SLA has already been designed, negotiation with a willing customer could be completed in three or four weeks – maybe even less depending on the complexity of the SLA. For a commercial customer, customers reluctant to embrace SLAs, or for the first pilot SLA, negotiation and implementation may take three to nine months elapsed time. (One commercial bureau service took over six months elapsed time and some nine man-months effort to implement their first SLA.) There can be a long lead time and high resource cost, especially for the first SLA.

4.14 Reporting actual performance against SLA

Periodic reports on achievement or non-achievement of SLA targets are necessary. The reporting timescale needs to be short enough not to average out significant under-performance and long enough not to deluge the service provider and customer in a stream of information. The more common options are:

- each accounting period
- each calendar month
- rolling four weeks
- rolling eight weeks.

The problem with accounting period or calendar monthly reporting is the cut-off: bad service spread over period end/period beginning could result in the achievement of SLA targets in each period, whereas had it not overlapped two reporting periods SLA targets could have been missed. A rolling reporting period is therefore preferable.

Reporting is aided by the use of a service database of performance information. If all incidents and problems resulting in service outages have been reported into the service database, it is relatively simple to produce SLA reports from it. However, the service database may have to be supplemented with performance information about background work, delivery performance, technical or professional support and other services. The schematic in Figure 4.7 shows a structure for SLA reporting founded on a service database:

- service outages are reported direct to a service provider from incident and problem reporting systems;
- deadlines missed are input;
- support services' missed targets are input;

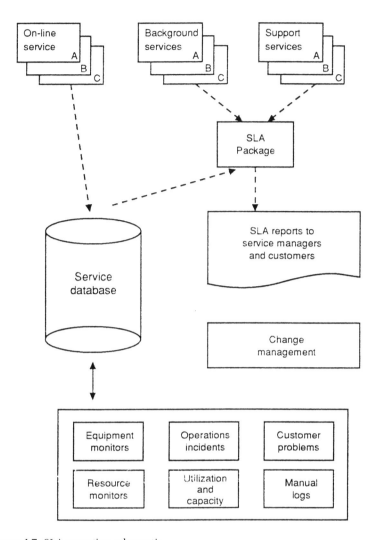

Figure 4.7 SLA reporting schematic.

- reports are provided to service provider management and to customers.

The shape and content of reports will vary depending on the type of SLA chosen. A look at a few examples of reports which are actually in use may help to show the variety of report types which can be used.

An SLA report could cover actual performance against targets in the following areas:

- availability
- response times
- turnround
- output arrangements
- throughput (volumes)
- help desk and customer care activity
- technical or professional support.

Month	Elapsed time	Service uptime hours	Service uptime per cent	Customer uptime hours	Customer uptime per cent total	Customer uptime per cent 0800–1800	Service breaks	Service outage* hours
			Service availability to customers for 199X	Monthly breakdown				
January	744.00	740.40	99.52%	727.71	87.81%	99.11%	3	3.60
February	696.00	696.00	100.00%	680.37	97.75%	99.92%	0	0.00
March	744.00	742.42	99.79%	726.74	97.47%	99.30%	2	1.58
April	720.00	717.25	99.62%	700.43	96.90%	99.63%	4	2.75
May	744.00	739.92	99.45%	725.16	96.92%	100.00%	1	4.08
June	720.00	719.78	99.97%	690.25	95.84%	100.00%	1	0.22
July	744.00	736.00	98.92%	724.04	96.24%	98.77%	3	8.00
August	744.00	726.31	97.62%	700.53	91.78%	100.00%	4	17.69
September	720.00	718.17	99.75%	705.22	97.69%	99.13%	1	1.83
October	528.00	527.16	99.84%	521.56	98.62%	99.21%	2	0.84

Service and customer availability uptime for 199X
Summary breakdown with percentages

Date of last record	Elapsed time	Service availability hours	Service availability per cent	Customer availability hours	Customer availability per cent	Customer availability 0800–1800	Service breaks	Service unavailability hours*
03.11.9X %	7368.00 100.00%	7327.4 99.45%	99.45%	7161.39 97.20%	96.64%	99.52%	21	40.59 0.55%

Mean time between failure for the previous 28 days = 672.00 hours

* Period of unavailability could be broken down further by cause.

Figure 4.8 Global service report – example.

In the event of any shortfall, the report should identify:

- time and duration of each failure
- number of failures
- reasons for failures
- similar information for partial failures.

At its simplest a report providing global uptime and service availability split between 'normal office hours' and 'other times' may be adequate (see Figure 4.8).

The sample SLA reports in Figures 4.9 and 4.10 take another approach. These refine reporting to specific services and reports on achievement and non-achievement of SLA targets. However, it may be necessary to differentiate between critical, prime and partial outages and cross-refer to a problem management system.

The graph in Figure 4.11 provides a method of measuring a particular service component – but the method could equally well be applied to the measurement of an entire service, with separate graphs for 'normal working hours', 'critical' and 'extended working hours' time regimes.

```
SERVICE LEVEL REPORT FOR SERVICE A

Week commencing: DD/MM/YY

The following is the service level performance extracted from the above service.
Please address any queries to the Service Manager, telephone 12345.
```

Services	SLA target %	Actual availability	SLA met Y/N	Cause	Date/time	Outage ddhhmm	Problem number
Service A	96.0	95.91	No	Staff shortage	ddmmyy 10.11	0:36	73422
				Staff shortage	ddmmyy 10.48	0:20	73412
				Staff shortage	ddmmyy 10.31	0:36	73422
				The following are partial outages:			
				Equipment	ddmmyy 11.20	0:40	73483

Figure 4.9 Sample SLA report.

Another way to measure the service provider's overall attainment of SLAs is to create a form of availability index (similar to the Financial Times All Share Index). The simplest would be to calculate:

$$\frac{\text{(Multiple of actual availabilities for period)}}{\text{(Multiple of all target availabilities for period)}} \times 1000$$

e.g. for four SLAs:

$$\frac{99.3}{99} \times \frac{98}{99} \times \frac{99.1}{98} \times \frac{94.5}{95} \times 1000 = 989.9$$

This figure could be used in trend graphs, newsletters or as staff achievement targets for management by objectives. (But should over-achievement on some SLAs be allowed to compensate for under-achievement on others?)

Output and reports	Deadlines missed								
	Mon	Tues	Wed	Thurs	Fri	Total	Allowed	All	Y/N
Reports 'A'	-	-	-	-	1	1	2	15	Y
Van despatch	-	-	-	-	-	-	1	60	Y
Reports 'B'	-	-	-	-	-	-	3	40	Y
Output '1'	-	-	-	-	-	-	1	5	Y
Reports 'C'	-	-	-	-	-	-	1	5	Y
Input 'X'	-	-	1	-	-	1	1	5	Y
Output '2'	-	-	1	-	1	2	1	45	N
Reports 'D'	-	-	-	-	-	-	1	5	Y
Input 'Y'	-	-	-	-	-	-	1	5	Y
Output 'AA'	-	-	-	-	1	1	1	5	Y
Output 'BB'	-	-	-	-	-	-	1	5	Y
Reports 'E'	-	-	-	-	-	-	1	5	Y

Figure 4.10 Background service level report (production type).

Percentage

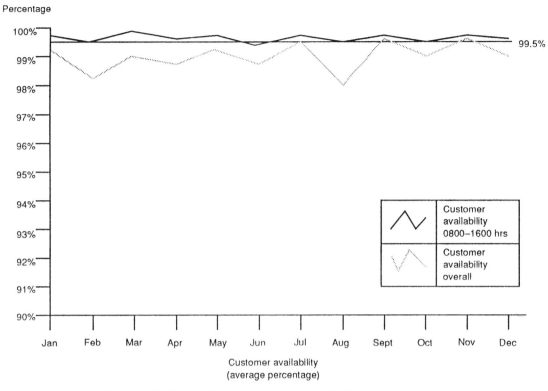

Figure 4.11 Service department – service availability.

4.15 Service review meetings

Service level data should be available for discussions at service review meetings. Typi-cally, separate service review meetings would be held with external:

- customers (jointly or individually)
- suppliers (chiefly maintenance vendors, bought-in services or contractors)

and with internal:

- customers
- suppliers
- accountants (concerning budget, cost and recovery)
- problem management teams
- change management teams
- capacity planning teams
- customer care and technical support teams.

These meetings will all seek to meet service level targets and help to establish what steps need to be taken in the event of shortfall (or substantial over-provision) of serv-ice quality, or in the light of changing business needs, whether to adjust the service or to adjust the SLA.

4.16 The customer review meeting

The frequency of meetings and seniority of attendees at the customer review meeting will depend upon:

- how mature the SLA is
- whether SLA targets are consistently being met
- the commercial value of the customer
- whether the SLA is due for renewal
- whether the customer wishes to negotiate changes to the SLA.

The normal attendees would be the customer account manager (supported by representatives from the appropriate areas and by the marketing and sales manager as appropriate) and the customer representative (supported if necessary by appropriate end-users of the service and by specialists).

A typical agenda might cover:

- minutes of previous meeting
- matters arising
- review of service performance against SLA:
  - availability
  - performance
  - utilization
  - background work
- report on help desk and customer care activity
- review of outstanding problems
- administrative issues
- planning:
  - proposed changes
  - requests for service enhancement
  - requests for new services or new service products
  - service changes (e.g. public holiday arrangements)
- adjustments to service or SLA
- any other business
- place, time and date of next meeting.

4.17 Service motivation

Service orientation does not just happen: individuals need to be motivated to make it happen. The organizational culture may dictate the motivational tools available to achieve a full service culture. Possible motivators could include:

- setting service targets as objectives for management by objectives (MBO) and reporting on achievement under annual appraisal systems
- linking performance pay to achievement of SLA objectives
- linking a group bonus to achievement of SLA objectives to encourage peer pressure against the less service-oriented individuals
- using service-orientation posters of the 'Customer is King' type

- immediate incentives for achievement (e.g. bottle of champagne for perfect service record for a month, league tables)
- making conduct which could jeopardize provision of service 'gross misconduct' – that is, a firing offence
- putting financial penalties on the service provider for non-achievement of SLAs (e.g. free re-runs so that the service provider's budget targets may be missed in the event of serious non-performance – with consequent post-mortems)

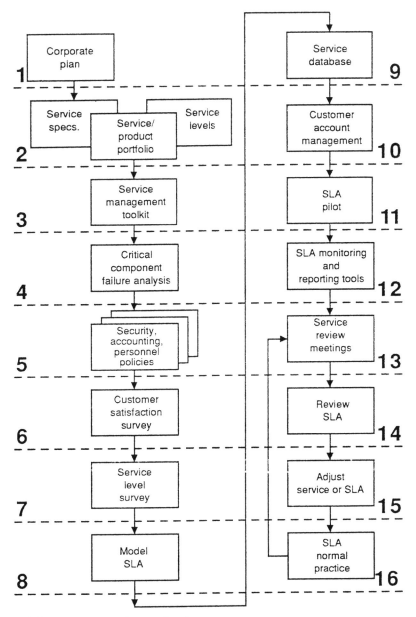

Figure 4.12 Components of service level management.

- putting financial or service quality penalties on customers who fail to deliver their forecast usage or fail to meet their side of the SLA
- instituting quality circles or other techniques to improve service quality.

4.18 Extending SLAs

When the period set for the pilot SLA trials is complete and the model SLA has been fine-tuned, SLAs can become normal practice for new customers and can be instituted in retrospect for existing customers – perhaps at the time charges are renegotiated or when budgets are renewed.

The components of service level management will now be in place (see Figure 4.12).

Service level survey

In order that we may assess and improve the service offered by the _____ service to our customers, we would be grateful if you would assist your customer account manager to complete the following questionnaire. A copy will then be forwarded to you for your records.

Customer details

Initials:

Surname:

Reference:

Site/Company:

Address:

Telephone No.:   Fax:

Date:

Service customer account manager details

Name:

Address:

Telephone No.:   Fax:

1. **Name of service:**
   Transaction or job delivery rates and response times
   Transaction or Job Name?

Transaction rates	RateTime/Day
How many per standard day?	
Per peak hour of day?	
Per peak hour of week?	
Per peak hour of month?	
Per peak hour of year?	

   Required response for this transaction type?
   (Alter percentages as required.)

90%	<	mins/hours/days
95%	<	mins/hours/days
99%	<	mins/hours/days

	+ 6 months	+ 1 year	+ 2 years
Projected % growth or decline	_____	_____	_____

   Other comments:

   (Please complete separate form for each type of transaction or job.)

2. Background jobs (production type)

(Day, time)

Input to services by:	
For turnround by:	
Output to:	
Despatch method:	
Security requirements:	
% missed deadlines acceptable:	

	+ 6 months	+ 1 year	+ 2 years
Projected % growth or decline	_____	_____	_____

Other comments:

(Please complete separate form for each type of transaction or job.)

3. Technical specification

Materials:

Standards:

Quality reference:

	+ 6 months	+ 1 year	+ 2 years
Projected % growth or decline	_____	_____	_____

Other comments:

Signed: _____ Customer

_____ Customer Account Manager

Terms of reference for marketing and sales manager

The marketing and sales manager is responsible for the overall effectiveness of the marketing section. The marketing manager monitors that customer account managers are undertaking the appropriate tasks assigned to them. The manager will undertake the following:

- review the market to identify prospective clients;
- seek to develop work from existing clients in conjunction with customer account managers;
- public relations;
- based on targets set for customer account manager, set targets for each marketing activity;
- compute results of marketing activities and monitor results against targets;
- ensure service level agreements (SLAs) are negotiated for each customer, monitor delivery of service against SLAs and provide details to customer account managers;
- monitor the customer account manager's progress.

Terms of reference for customer account managers

Customer account managers will be responsible for monitoring the success of the _____ service in providing their customers with the service they require in accordance with contracts and service level agreements. They will be responsible for identifying customer needs and relaying those to executive areas of the _____ service; identifying areas of customer concern and initiating action to resolve the issues which give rise to that concern; identifying customer needs and relating these to services which the _____ service can provide, thus expanding business with that customer.

Customer account managers will take the following activities:

- by personal initiatives and by working with the marketing and sales manager, promote _____ services so as to assist the marketing and sales manager close sales;
- identify and advise the marketing and sales manager of any possible new areas of business;
- identify areas of industry research required and passing these to the marketing and sales manager for action;
- monitor service to the customers against contracts or service level agreements (SLAs), identifying and resolving any shortfall;
- manage customer demand as far as possible so as to avoid peaking of work for the _____ services;
- review customer usage against contract (or SLA), identifying over- or under-fulfilment and informing the _____ service manager of its implications, and liaising with the customer on under- or over-fulfilment against contract or SLA;
- make regular visits to customers to a schedule agreed with the marketing and sales manager;

- make interim telephone calls to customers between visits to identify and defuse any areas of concern and to promote the further use of the _____ service;
- arrange for visits to the _____ service by prospects and customers for discussions on optimizing the value of the _____ service to them;
- arrange visits to the _____ service by customers for familiarization or to use facilities available;
- coordinate the _____ service resources to facilitate transfer of customer work to it;
- in consultation with other managers within the _____ service, coordinate logistics to ensure that customers are able to access the services they require at the time they require;
- in consultation with other managers within the _____ service, ensure that both the _____ service and customer security is protected;
- arrange customer attendance at appropriate seminars, exhibitions, workshops, presentations, etc., recommended by or provided by the marketing and sales manager;
- identify customer training needs relevant to the _____ service and liaise with the customer support manager to meet these needs;
- identify any unsatisfied requirements of the customer for documentation or publications which the _____ service is required to provide and satisfy their requirements;
- monitor the duration of the contract or SLA and ensure that all possible efforts are made to ensure continuation of provision of the _____ service to the customer;
- provide regular reports to the operational managers within the _____ service and early advice of the cessation of or renewal of any contract or SLA;
- advise the marketing and sales manager of any possible new areas of business and participate in planning of customer account development.

The downside risk, alternatives to service level agreements and the SLA payoff

5.1 SLAs: reasons for failure

Not every SLA implementation is a success story. The possibility of failure has to be acknowledged. If the climate is not right for SLAs it might be preferable to consider implementing an alternative method to achieve at least partially the same ends.

But before admitting defeat, it may help to consider why SLA implementations fail. They fail because:

- the business has no clear mission or direction;
- the SLAs have no clear aim or direction;
- the business application has no identifiable or accountable 'owner' or 'sponsor';
- the owner can't – or won't – see the benefits (they may later, if benefits are provided by other SLAs);
- service definitions are vague, they do not cover the whole service to the end-user's desk, or they are not aligned to SLA aims or measurement processes;
- SLAs have not been tailored to meet business needs (the relevant SLA objective may have been missed, e.g. by concentrating on accuracy rather than on timeliness);
- implementation spade-work has not been done: the ESCRIT framework is not in place (the text of the SLA is not supported by an adequate infrastructure);
- SLAs do not specify clear targets;
- SLAs specify impractical, vague or unachievable targets;
- the SLA is too detailed, cumbersome, indigestible and difficult to monitor;
- the SLA is too skimpy and does not contain enough service criteria to be taken seriously;
- the targets which are specified omit key factors so that, although the targets are met, they are not comprehensive enough to deliver appropriate service quality;
- the SLA has not been followed up by real service orientation: it merely pays lip service to the concept;

- measurements are too comprehensive and SLA monitoring is swamped with detail;
- monitoring has been inadequate and missed problem areas;
- monitoring is not perceived by the customer as being objective and impartial;
- service level management has not been sufficiently resourced with:
  - skills
  - staff (head-count)
  - finance
  - the service level management toolkit;
- the SLA project lacks control:
  - management is insufficiently involved
  - problems are not effectively followed up
  - service review meetings have withered
  - service has foundered on political in-fighting within the service department;
- no sanctions are applied for missing targets;
- no effective remedial action is taken when targets are missed.

To implement service level agreements the whole of the service department must speak with one voice and present one face to the customer.

5.2 Alternatives to SLAs

What alternatives to SLAs are there? Most alternatives fail to create a true meeting of minds between customer and the service provider, do not promote service culture as effectively and do not align the service business needs as directly as SLAs do. However, corporate culture may prevent the effective implementation of SLAs. If SLAs are not practicable within an organization the service management disciplines and methodologies discussed earlier should nevertheless improve service provision. Other options are:

- performance indicators
- availability and response targets, which may be:
  - implicit
  - explicit
  - standard
  - model
- benchmark checks
- customer satisfaction surveys.

5.3 Performance indicators

Performance indicators may be published and circulated to customers (possibly in a newsletter) or discussed at customer service review meetings.

Current performance may be compared with past performance, perhaps by means of a trend graph, so customers can see whether service is consistent, improving or declining.

Performance indicators have their drawbacks. They are implicitly a one-way contract: the customer may not be tied to volume or throughput forecasts or to meeting deadlines, yet implicitly the service provider is expected to deliver consistent service levels.

Performance indicators may cover:

- equipment faults:
  - MTBF, MTTF downtime by day/hour, number of customers impacted and cost of impact
- other faults impacting on service:
  - downtime by day/hour and number of customers impacted
- total problems:
  - number, severity and time to rectify
- response time:
  - by type of job or transaction
- job completion:
  - time in various categories
- utilization and capacity:
  - forecast versus actual
- output:
  - against accuracy targets
  - against target deadlines
  - effectiveness (did it achieve or provide what the customer wanted?)
- delivery mechanisms:
  - against target deadlines
  - against in-transit defect targets.

5.4 Availability and response targets

5.4.1 Implicit

The accounts department may have a regular task of producing financial management information. Although no formal targets have been set, the accounts department knows that the later the results are produced, the less their value. It therefore aims to produce the output by the third working day of each period. It depends on the computing service to provide computing capacity but even if there is a computer breakdown the accounts department makes every effort to produce the output on time. In this case, implicit targets have been established by custom and practice.

Similarly with response. Where no formal response targets have been set, a customer may phone the information desk to complain that they have not yet received product information requested three days ago. If the information desk agrees that this response is 'slow', it implies a response target that is better.

Implicit targets are common as an organization embraces a service for the first time, while the service is immature. But implicit response targets are an abdication of responsibility and can only ultimately lead to dissatisfaction of both customer and service provider. There are no substitutes for service management.

5.4.2 Explicit

Explicit targets are frequently one-sided. They may be designated by the service provider as 'reasonable'.

They may be expressed in terms of availability:

'The cash office will be open from 1100 hours to 1400 hours Monday to Friday.'

in terms of response:

'In the event of a fire alarm sounding the fire service will attend the scene within four minutes.'

in terms of accuracy:

'Calculations will be performed to three decimal places, rounded up.'

in terms of defect rate:

'The maintenance service should not experience more than two call-backs per week.'

or by other appropriate measurements.

Alternatively, explicit requirements may be imposed by the organization on the service provider:

'Payslips will be produced for circulation by 0800 hours on the last Friday of each month. Salary payroll tapes will be sent to Clearers so as to arrive by 1600 hours on the last Friday of each month.'

or:

'75% of customers' letters will be answered the same day, 95% within three working days and 100% within five working days even if this means sending an interim reply.'

Explicit targets may be expressed in a service specification for a new service product to be handled by existing resources which are already heavily loaded, and the service provider may not have been a party to the specification process – clearly an untenable situation.

5.4.3 Standard

Standard targets are often used by bureaux. They may state the terms and conditions on which work is to be undertaken (usually with the implication that they are not negotiable, although in practice they may be). Standard targets may impose obligations on both customer and service provider. Again, payroll is a good example:

'The customer will provide completed input by 1200 hours on the last Wednesday of each month for a payday of the last Friday in the month.'

5.4.4 Model

Model targets are usually the performance indicators (and perhaps explicit service level targets) set by the service provider but they are declared to the customer and represent a framework within which the customer and the service provider may negotiate. This negotiation may, for instance, involve improving response by changing job priority – perhaps involving overtime working – at a consequently higher cost to the customer.

Equally the negotiation could result in the customer bringing forward the deadline for completion of output, or smoothing work over a longer period. Model targets are the closest to SLAs in that a dialogue involving negotiation is established between customer and service provider.

5.5 Benchmark checks

The benchmark approach involves taking several typical or representative jobs (a 'basket'), establishing response time service level targets for completion of them, and periodically checking that this has been achieved. Taken in conjunction with model availability targets and model or explicit background job targets they can make a substantial contribution to service level management without an SLA, or they may be included as part of an SLA.

Benchmark checks are particularly useful for 'difficult to measure' services involving a varied workload of small jobs – maybe an in-house print or reprographic service.

This could involve sampling job cards to establish how long it took to deliver, for example:

- 100 visiting cards
- three reams of printed stationery
- a photocopying request for a 100 page document
- binding of 50 reports.

Although the detail of the work and the customer's need for it may vary from week to week, the type of job may be fairly constant.

5.6 Business satisfaction analysis

We have seen how a customer satisfaction survey (at the end of Chapter 2) can provide a base line from which to measure the customer's perception of the quality of the service. We have also seen how a service level survey (at the end of Chapter 4), completed by the customer with help from a representative of the IT department, can provide detail on which an SLA can be based. Some organizations go further and use business satisfaction analysis techniques instead of SLAs. They start with a formal business analysis process which relates both the customer's and the service provider's objectives to corporate goals.

The customer satisfaction survey may be used to identify the customer's perception of the value of the service.

This is followed by a full-scale review of all of the service provider's offerings to its customers. The service provider will have a range of service products. It may also be providing standard reports, installation services maintenance and help desk. It will be operating various procedures (perhaps for change management, for ordering equipment, for booking time or for requests for new services). The service provider will operate a number of processes (examples include production of microfiches, printing, binding and database updating). It may also run a number of systems (that is, operational systems supporting the service run on dedicated or specific, identifiable equipment).

All these products, services, procedures, processes and systems should be evaluated against the actual needs of the customers in fulfilling their contribution to corporate objectives.

Information analysis techniques may then be used to identify the relevance, timeliness and value of all the service provider's activities in contributing to the achievement of corporate plans.

In the mature service many activities result from history rather than need. Many services are provided in a particular way or to a particular format because that was the easiest way of meeting what was expressed as a customer need at the time. The business analysis process gives the opportunity to identify what the present need really is and how well it is met by present services.

The business satisfaction analysis may be repeated annually to ensure that the service maintains appropriate quality and relevance to the business.

This type of business satisfaction analysis represents a thorough audit of the value of all the work of the service provider. It should identify all those activities which are of little value or relevance and help to adjust priorities so that resources can be allocated to key areas. This approach may in fact achieve more than SLAs taken in isolation since it provides an opportunity to rank all the service provider's activities in order of importance. The benefits of business satisfaction analysis are that:

- it aligns the service to business needs;
- it leads to better utilization of the assets used by the service;
- it emphasizes the value of what is produced rather than the mechanics of producing it;
- it improves the effectiveness of the service by identifying non-essential activities;
- it involves the customer orientation of the service;
- it increases customer satisfaction;
- it monitors customer satisfaction.

The service management toolkit is as important in this scenario as for SLAs, and the analysis has to have sufficient management support to ensure that any recommendations for change are followed through. The recommendations may involve changes in either the customer's area or the service provider's.

Whereas the SLA is an excellent vehicle where there is substantial departmental autonomy or in a decentralized environment, the business satisfaction analysis can be very appropriate for an organization with a strong centralized culture.

5.7 The SLA payoff: success stories

Although reasons for failure have been examined, it is encouraging to be able to finish on a couple of success stories.

A large distribution company had experienced considerable growth and was bursting out of its existing high-quality office accommodation. The organization decided to introduce SLAs in a number of service areas, one of them being office services. Because the organization had a history of reorganization and change, its office services team maintained several stores of furniture at various locations so they could react quickly to new requirements. One of the stores was in a basement, another was in office accommodation in a headquarters building.

A customer satisfaction analysis showed that, despite the stores, the customers of the office services were dissatisfied with response and choice of furniture. The reason for poor response was that office services relied on the transport section to deliver the furniture, and the transport section's priorities were to external customers rather than internal ones.

An attempt at an SLA identified these conflicts and a business satisfaction analysis identified a mismatch between business needs and the traditional office services function.

The accommodation problems – the real issues – were resolved by discontinuing the furniture stores and releasing:

- prime office accommodation
- basement space to which the computer equipment could be relocated as a darkroom operation, thus releasing further office space vacated by the consequential move of the computer centre.

The office furniture service was redesigned to use just-in-time call-out from a supplier who contracted to deliver within SLA timescales from a defined catalogue. This:

- saved office furniture inventory costs
- resolved the priority conflict on the transport section, since furniture deliveries were made by the supplier
- released internal furniture 'warehousemen' or 'heavy gang' staff for more productive duties
- reduced the administrative costs associated with management of the in-house furniture inventory
- provided a wider choice of office furniture to the in-house customer, while containing unit costs within agreed limits.

The saving from this exercise totalled some £350,000 a year – but more important was the fact that the accommodation problem was solved without having to move outside the central complex, with associated productivity benefits. An added bonus was that in-house customers perceived that the office services section was providing a greatly improved service against agreed service levels.

Another success story concerns a dynamically growing telecommunications company which operated a service desk. While the service desk did its best to provide a friendly and responsive service, its success or failure was not very well quantified and internal management, external customers and the sales and marketing staff at the company expected more from it than it was able to provide. As a result of defining service level requirements, an investment was made in tools to support the service desk. The service desk can now fix up to 98% of problems over the telephone with an average response time to fix of some 12 minutes. Because much of the work has now been automated, problem escalation is much more efficient and effective. The system incorporates information on call status and ensures that customers' calls get answered in order of priority and arrival. Not only this, but they have the tools in place to identify trends in their particular market-place and to produce information on the reliability of their products in the field. They can also identify strengths and weaknesses of their engineers and areas where training is required. The service level requirement for the service desk led to centralization of information on contracts, maintenance and warranty. Contract handling has been improved and the service desk now provides the marketing and sales teams with competitive-edge support to boost sales.

5.8 Where next?

The need for business-orientated utility services will inevitably lead to automation of many of the service management functions. In telecommunications, manual switching gave way to mechanical and subsequently electronic switching and we are now in the era of dynamic network management using intelligent software. In exactly the same way many service functions will inevitably become automated to reduce human error and increase cost-effective quality and consistency of service.

It is not difficult to envisage the present generation of computer systems which support our services to be extended to include:

- automatic alarm when errors are discovered
- automatic rectification of error conditions
- automatic escalation of errors or problems
- automatic reporting of failure to meet SLA targets
- links to disaster recovery and business continuity planning arrangements providing automatic call-out or even automatic invocation of stand-by arrangements
- automatic production of SLA performance reports.

5.9 Conclusion

There are alternatives to SLAs, but only SLAs get the message across that the service provider is embracing the full service culture. SLAs can help to align service functions with business needs, but they cannot be effectively implemented without the service management toolkit being in place, without adequate resources and without commitment from all involved. And once involved, they continue to need servicing.

But for how long? This book started by saying that in-house services were being treated as just another utility. We have devoted many words to discussing SLAs — but we don't usually have specific service level agreements with utilities. There is a general implicit service level of 100% availability and immediate response. If our in-house services are defect-free, why do we need SLAs? But are they truly defect free? Most of the utilities have taken a century to get to their present level of quality and reliability – and they still get complaints! And even if our services are defect free, how do we know the quality is appropriate to business needs? Even when it is, we will need the service level toolkit for internal management of the service. We cannot afford to wait for the future – we need SLAs now!

6

Case study: service level agreements in construction management

6.1 Introduction

Of all services that are provided, management services are one of the purest, in the sense that no tangible product is being contracted for – only the service of managing.

Construction management is an example of management services. The construction manager is employed by a client who wishes to undertake a construction project to manage the project on behalf of the client employer.

In a large number of (if not most) projects the issue of measurement of the services being provided by the manager receives little or no contractual treatment. This inevitably creates potential for discrepancies in the services which are provided and, in the worst cases, fuels disputes.

This chapter focuses on the potential use of service levels in the context of construction management to examine the approaches that could be adopted, the points of issue and the benefits that may accrue. The purpose of the chapter is to provide a basis for discussion based on example, rather than attempting to prescribe any one recommended approach. Any similarity between examples given and any factual case is, of course, unintended and no reference to specific cases is to be drawn or implied.

The discussion begins with a background for readers who may be unfamiliar with the development of contractual bases for construction projects and terminology used where the management of the project is not undertaken by the employer. It then goes on to examine a typical approach and, finally, outlines and discusses a service level oriented approach to construction management.

6.2 Background

In the procurement of construction projects a number of approaches to the management of the procurement and the project itself have evolved. This chapter will focus on one only, construction management, which has the greatest degree of analogy to a service provision paradigm when compared with other forms of construction contracting.

It will be helpful to an understanding of the analysis and suggested application of service level agreement methods that follows to cover first some background to the development of construction management.

In periods of high inflation and when there is a premium in commencing work expeditiously on site, traditional approaches to construction contracting are inadequate. To help remedy this, in some cases employers adopted a contractual framework known as management contracting, under which the employer wishing to have a building built would contract with one contractor who would in turn contract with all the trade contractors (the employer would have separate arrangements with the design team for the project). Often management contracting would be undertaken on a cost basis which left the employer to meet the cost of any overrun on the project.

Management contracting became established in the UK as early as the 1960s. In 1983 the Construction Industry Research and Information Association published its 100th Report 'Management Contracting' on this form of contracting, by which time it had come to represent to many employers the means to achieve greater speed and cost control in construction projects.

Management contracting gave the employer simplicity in the contracting process and a framework that appeared to give greater assurance, by having one substantial contracting party to sue in the event of a default under the contract, without requiring the employer to become involved in pursuing obligations among many smaller trade contractors involved.

However, management contracting tends not to encourage a sympathetic or partnership spirit between the employer and the management contractors, as the contract is frequently biased to load obligations and liabilities onto the management contractor. Also the apparent simplicity of the framework leaves uncertain much of the detail of control of cost and management of change which the contracting process almost inevitably requires.

Dissatisfaction with the tendency to an adversarial nature of management contracting in the construction industry led employers and contractors to look for a contracting framework that would better accommodate the need for cooperation and rapid progress in a modern construction project.

Construction management developed as a response to this dissatisfaction It preserves the direct contractual relationship of a construction employer with the trade contractors on the project. Instead of interposing a single contractor to provide the construction management services required to execute the project, the employer enters into a separate agreement with a construction manager.

As an aside, note that 'works package contractors' (in the management contract context) and 'trade contractors' (in construction management) both refer to what, in more traditional forms of contracting, would be known as subcontractors.

Experience has shown that construction management may not represent in any sense a total solution to the question of construction procurement for all projects. The need, if disputes arise, for the employer to deal directly with what, on a large project, can be literally hundreds of trade contractors can in practice be a major disadvantage. In any event, the perceived tendency to an adversarial situation in management contracting may not be anything like as real as has been suggested.

The truth of the matter is, as to be expected, that it is a question of selecting the most appropriate method of procurement for each project. Given the particular needs and skills of the employer, and the level of risk which he is able or wishes to bear, how is the project most likely to be taken from inception to successful completion?

Within this context, construction management undoubtedly represents a popular basis for contracting, and the one in which the provision of services is most obviously the principle objective of the contract.

6.3 Construction management – typical approach

As explained above, construction management avoids a contracting framework where only one contractor is responsible directly to the employer for all aspects of the construction process (and subcontracts separate tasks to trade contractors). In construction management the employer contracts with one manager to provide the management services required to coordinate and supply the infrastructure required for the management of the construction project. In its simplest terms a construction management agreement therefore constitutes an agreement for the provision of services (management of the construction project) by the manager to the employer.

As such, construction management provides an area of contracting in which the principles of service level management and service level agreements may usefully be examined for the contribution that their application could make to the improvement of the contracting process.

It might be said that the same is true for management contracting. The important difference, and the reason why construction management has been selected for the present exercise, is that the interposition of the management contractor in the contractual chain between the employer and the works package contractors means that the management contracts have to deal with much more than the provision of services.

Typically, management contracts contain quite complex arrangements for the allocation of the risks of, for example, default and insolvency of the works package contractors. Construction management contracts generally do not have to address such matters. In that sense, they are therefore a purer form of service agreement.

Nonetheless, the essential service element of a management contract means that much of what follows may be as applicable for management contracts as it is for construction management.

A typical construction management agreement will set out provisions under which are the detailed obligations of the construction manager as prescribed. For example, a construction management agreement may identify two phases to the provision of management services, namely:

- pre-project services, and
- project implementation services.

Within each phase are a number of processes and products which will be covered.

6.3.1 Pre-project services

- Design related services: for example, reviewing employer's requirements, and commenting on and discussing these with the employer and other professional parties engaged by the employer.
- Preparing a specification, or procuring the preparation of a specification (by others), for the project or for particular aspects of the project.
- Monitoring the integrity or 'buildability' of the project planning at the design stage.
- Cost planning, including preparing detailed cash flow projects.
- Carrying out preparatory work, including obtaining approvals from third-party bodies and organizations, coordinating bids, preparing project plans.
- Coordinating bids and organizing and operating the bid procedure.

6.3.2 Project implementation services

- Providing infrastructure for the project management (e.g. accommodation, office equipment and staffing).
- Surveying the site and establishing base lines.
- Planning agreements, plans and other documents.
- Issuing instructions to and receiving applications for payment for trade contractors, etc.
- Coordinating project work.
- Organizing progress meetings with the employer and other contracting parties.
- Operating cost control procedures.
- Operating change control procedures.
- Monitoring compliance with legislative requirements.
- Monitoring performance to specification and project plan.
- Recording project progress and other aspects requiring monitoring.
- Undertaking insurance.

6.4 Construction management – service-oriented approach

Examination of the typical approach to construction management contracting shows that there is a great emphasis in the form of agreement on provisions covering the 'what' of the management services to be provided but significantly little coverage of the 'how'.

Applying a service level management approach to the provision of construction management services could address this lack in an important area of the process of construction management and should assist in the improvement of the quality of the services and the effectiveness of the contract for both parties.

The need for an approach that addresses the 'how' of the provision of services, in the context of management contracting, has been contemplated in an SERC report *Roles, Responsibilities and Risks in Management Contracts* (Professor C.D. Chapman, S.C. Ward and Dr M. McDonald). In their consideration of the basis for assessment of project performance and the desire to improve effectiveness they anticipate there will be practical difficulties, if all that is sought is the measurement of effectiveness by reference to the attainment of ultimate goals set down at the beginning of the project (Chapter 7, page 22, of the report).

Clearly, if any method of measuring and controlling the provision of services in construction management is to be effective, there must be frequent opportunities to assess progress and levels of service achieved. The SERC report suggests that '[employees] need to... specify not just the tasks or objectives they are trying to accomplish, but also the **processes** that are involved in accomplishing them.' The authors propose a 'system needs' approach for understanding and improving organization processes.

This approach treats the whole construction project as a system and identifies the needs of that system, as set out in a study (Georgopoulos, 1973) identifying headings for 'systems needs' of:

- adaptation – ability to adapt favourably to environment changes
- allocation – ability to deploy and allocate resources in the most appropriate manner
- coordination – of energies and efforts to the solution of the system's problems and objectives
- integration – of individual members to develop common organization values and share norms
- tension management – ability to minimize and resolve tensions and conflicts
- productivity/integrity – ability to preserve identity and integrity as a distinct problem-solving system regardless of changes occurring inside and outside the system.

Whilst this approach gives a useful perspective at the level of the whole project, and underlines the importance of measures in the contracting process which address these needs, the measures by which the needs are to be met require exploration.

6.5 Service levels in construction management

To adopt a service level management approach (and to prepare service level agreements) in relation to the construction management process, a method for analysis of the processes and products involved in the management of construction projects is required which makes identification of the services involved (as processes and products) amenable to the next stage, namely the implementation of management service metrics.

The areas of activity involved in construction management can be categorized under headings which may usefully be described as process and 'work product' types:

6.5.1 Liaison/recording

- Canvassing of views/position of third parties, inspections.
- Instructing/taking instructions.
- Reporting on monitored processes and products.
- Operating formal liaison procedures (change control/cost controls/dispute resolution).

6.5.2 Monitoring/records

- Conformance to specifications/regulations/legislation.
- Deviation from specifications/timetable/project plan.
- Progress.
- Extraneous factors/developments.
- Costs.

6.5.3 Programme

- Prepare plans required/procure plans.
- Coordinate implementation of plans.
- Changes.

6.5.4 Advise/decide

- Action/design.
- Predicted effect/risk.
- Liability/interpretation.

6.5.5 Procure/provide

- Materials.
- Resources (human or other).
- Documentation.
- Plans (executed or otherwise).

The above constitutes the application of a semantic analysis to the processes and 'products' covered by provisions contained in the construction management agreement. This provides a framework from which to apply service level metrics as appropriate to the construction management services being provided.

It would not be appropriate in many cases to apply measurement to each of the possible areas of activity of the construction manager. By prioritizing those areas in which a service level agreement (or similar service level procedure) could be operated, we may anticipate the greatest benefit in improvement of effectiveness and quality of the services provided and progress towards ensuring considerable gains in the execution of the project itself.

Before considering possible prime target services it is worth touching on the basis on which such service level agreements could be measured in practice.

The options are: for the construction manager to measure its own service level achievement, for the employer to provide such measurement itself, or for an independent party to be commissioned by the employer. In many circumstances the provision by the construction manager of a separate individual or group to perform the service measurement function will be satisfactory to the employer. Alternatively, in more substantial agreements, the employer may already engage a professional team or its members in a capacity similar to that required for service level monitoring and the involvement of the relevant members of the professional team in this process will be to provide a more focused role than exists under current practice.

It is to be anticipated that a combination of self-measurement and independent measurement will be the most cost-effective solution. Any construction manager operating to recognized quality assurance methods will be involved in an exercise of a similar nature and, therefore, the cost of making available to the employer the information outputs of internal quality procedures will not be as great as would be required if a new system had to be introduced to support the service level measurement required.

The areas that we will look at for the purpose of this example as providing the greatest return from the adoption of service level measurement would be:

- liaison (reporting on monitored processes, products and costs)
- monitoring (performance and deviation)
- programming (coordination and implementation).

It should be stressed that there is an argument for an overall approach to be adopted in which the entire service level matrix for the construction management services is treated to continuing and regular review with service level review meetings.

6.6 Service levels in construction management – identifying metrics for management services

It is vital to the effectiveness of any service level framework applied to construction management that it will have (or is believed to have) consistency of effect even when tested legally.

Achieving this requires that we ask what the intended effect of a service level agreement is. Assuming that the prime effect desired is the provision of a means with which to measure and assure the attributes of the services being provided, the corollary of any failure to meet an agreed level must be some compensation to the employer.

When considering the measure of compensation, it is important to distinguish between:

- compensation for the lack of a service that had been agreed to
- the loss or damage, if any, that may be a result of the lack of service in question.

If compensation for the first exceeds an amount which is based on a 'refund' of some part of the fee for the service, then it will be presumed that the compensation includes an element of a pre-estimate of the loss arising from the lack of service, or, if no reasonable pre-estimate of loss can be argued, the compensation is in fact a penalty.

If the compensation is considered to be a pre-estimate of loss then there is a risk that additional loss arising from the lack of service will not be recoverable. If the compensation prescribed by the agreement is held to be a penalty then the amount that constitutes a penalty will not be recoverable.

We would suggest, therefore, that any compensation for lack of service determined under the service level agreement must be evaluated and carefully framed to take effect as an adjustment of a reasonably attributable amount of the fee for the service or as a reasonable (and legally tenable) pre-estimate of loss (often referred to by the somewhat negative term 'liquidated damages').

Without a sound basis in law a service level agreement will only give the appearance of assuring the service provided. On the simplest level, construction management means that the manager is employed to manage the construction of the building, not to provide the building itself. Although liability may arise from neglect in the service of management provided, the only adjustment that can be regulated within a service level agreement is confined to the amount paid for the service.

To illustrate these points let us take a hypothetical example. If service level management is deployed in respect of the services provided by the construction manager, the fact of a set of defective windows being installed, for example, gives rise to no lack of service merely from the fact of the windows being defective. If, under the service level agreement, no measurable lack of service incident had occurred in connection with the installation of the defective windows, then there will be no adjustment of the construction manager's fee. There may be loss or damage arising from the defective windows, but the compensation that the employer may recover will not be governed by the service level management procedures under the service level agreement.

However, if the installation of defective windows would have been detected by the proper execution of the construction manager's duties under the service level agreement, such as an inspection or test of the windows, then the employer should, it is suggested, be entitled under the service level agreement to an adjustment of the fee in its favour. This arises on the basis that a service, in this case an inspection, should have been provided under the contract, but was not provided, and so the amount of the construction manager's fee which can be attributed to the inspection should not be payable.

Of course, in the example given, the adjustment of the fee compensates for the lack of the service that should have been provided, but does not attempt (as we argue it must not) to deal with the question of what and how much compensation the employer should be entitled to recover, and from whom, when the defects in the windows are discovered.

If a service level agreement had been in place which required as mandatory items for the technical project team meeting status reports on all works backed by inspection and test data, the absence of the relevant report (or, less likely, the report that the inspection had not been carried out) would provide the opportunity for correction of the problem at the earliest opportunity. This is, it is suggested, the practical benefit of adopting service level management in such a project.

It would increase the value of adopting the service level management, for the employer, if the occurrence of any specified lack of service, by reference to the service level agreement, is expressed in the contract for the service to be prima facie evidence of negligence on the part of the person responsible for the service in question.

Turning to the measurement of construction management service, we focus on the areas of liaison, monitoring and programming.

Following the headings in the analysis given above, what would be the basis for measurement of the construction manager's service in canvassing the views and position of third parties with respect to the construction project and the carrying out of inspections?

One approach to the measurement of such services would be to duplicate the service either through an independent third party checking what was done, or by the employer carrying out the checking itself. The cost of duplicating effort at this level is unlikely to be economic for the employer, unless supervening factors, such as safety, require it.

An approach which should incur modest additional cost, or no cost if the construction manager is already deploying a methodology which generates these outputs, will be the specification in the service level agreement of the reports and their subject matter to be provided to the employer during the services categorized above.

In the context of canvassing views of third parties affected by the project, one would expect to see a specification that required a report to be provided, before a specified date in the project programme, which set out as mandatory subject matter (even if the text appearing in the resulting report would be 'none relevant'):

- the identities and interests of all parties which are affected by the project
- relevant regulations and legislative requirements affecting interaction with third parties affected by the project
- the manager's recommendations for action or otherwise in respect of each of the affected parties, with reasons
- actions etc. taken to date by the manager under contractual powers on behalf of the employer.

During the progress of the project updates of this report itself could be an agenda item for the relevant team meetings of the employer and construction manager, and, if so, this should be prescribed by the service level agreement. In effect, the meetings of the project teams, constituted with members from the employer and the construction manager will be service level review meetings, within the context of the service level agreement. These meetings will have the role of identifying and fixing the level of service being provided, by reference to criteria such as those discussed here, and operating the contractual procedures which relate to management of the services in the service level agreement.

Taking instructions from and reporting on instructions given by the employer are central to the services provided to the employer. Under a service level agreement these activities should specify as appropriate to the size and nature of the project:

- a project team or teams
- the make-up (by number, position and in some cases experience and qualifications) of the project team
- timetabling criteria for meetings of the project team(s)
- mandatory subject matter for the agenda for the team meetings
- mandatory reports to be generated for team meetings, with timing and details of circulation
- powers and responsibilities of project team members on behalf of the respective parties.[1]

Mandatory agenda items would include the reporting of decisions taken by the manager under contractually delegated powers on behalf of the client, with reasoning and background as required in the context of the project and specified in the service level agreement.

It will be apparent that the approach described involves specifying the outputs of the 'work product' or 'service product' types identified in the previous section. In information technology services an analogous reference would often be to 'service lines'.

Measuring lack of service in the provision of any 'service product' in construction management must be by reference to a simple yardstick, or the application of the measurement will itself prove too difficult to be of practical value. In the case of the service of taking and reporting on instructions by the construction manager, it is suggested that the event of any report as identified in the service level agreement not being provided at the required time or with incomplete or inaccurate content will be an event giving rise to some entitlement on the part of the employer to compensation by way of adjustment of fee. A single event need not give rise to compensation, of course, but the occurrence of the event will make an increment towards any compensatory provision that the parties agree in the service level agreement, if sufficient events occur.

It will be noted that inaccuracy in a report is suggested as the basis for an event giving rise to compensation. How will the inaccuracy be detected? As suggested in the sections above, the degree to which the employer requires independent verification of the service being provided will determine whether or not an independent third party is employed to carry out such work. If verification is required, effective coverage can often be achieved with statistically based selective checks on activities, without the checking of all work, with its attendant costs, being required.

---

1. To simplify the example 'reports' have been used in their widest sense and would include, for example, a response by the construction manager to a change request raised by the employer, which could fail to be considered by a number of differently constituted project teams in a large project in relation to their areas of responsibility, such as design, technical and finance mangement project teams.

In the area of programming and sequencing of the project, a similar approach would require that the service level agreement specify the various levels of programme which the construction manager would be required to prepare and update at relevant stages in the project. Depending on the complexity of the project, provision for sub-programmes would be necessary where a multi-phase multi-subcontractor programme is being undertaken. The production and updating of programmes, and the reporting of events and causes which would necessitate changes in any programme, would also be a mandatory subject matter item for the agenda of the project team meetings specified in the service level agreement.

The operation of an effective change control procedure (allied, one assumes it goes without saying, to a cost control procedure) will form a key part of the service level management framework. The principle that the project is described by the specifications, design documents and the programmes and that changes to any part of these must be carried out through a contractually specified change control mechanism is as much a pre-requisite to control of the project as it is to the use of service level management, which provides a tool to make the business of managing the project precise and effective.

Appendix A: service level agreement checklist

This checklist is intended to assist in the development of a service level agreement. Since service level agreements can be used to describe a variety of services, the elements appropriate to any specific SLA will depend on the circumstances.

The checklist, though long, is by no means exhaustive but is intended to help the reader to identify aspects relevant to their particular service environment. An SLA including all these items would be cumbersome and impractical. It is therefore not intended that all items should be included in an SLA, only that all items should be considered. Some of them may be reflected in job descriptions, in management by objectives targets, in relationships between customer care staff and customer, or between one service department and another.

Grateful acknowledgements are due to George W. (Bill) Miller, American Airlines (see Bibliography) from whose work this checklist has been developed. Any aberrations are the author's, not Bill Miller's!

Service level agreement checklist

Purpose of agreement

Date of effect

Duration of agreement

Parties to agreement
Service manager
Site/accommodation/facilities manager
Service customer account manager
Customer sites/accommodation manager
Customer contacts

Description of service
Overview and objectives
Site(s) to which service is to be provided
Definition of service:

- Definition of service regimes:
  - normal working day
  - extended working day

- prime time
- peak time
- non-prime time
- weekend/public holidays
- Background services (routine production-type services):
  - specify and describe each service product
  - including ancillary support requirements
  - and output requirements
- Real-time services:
  - specify and describe each service product
  - including ancillary requirements
- Delivery mechanisms:
  - delivery mechanisms and telecommunications
    - voice
    - fax/telex
    - teletext/ceefax
    - data
    - video
    - courier
    - equipment provision
    - equipment maintenance
    - transport
- Facilities management services:
  - equipment covered
  - operations provided
  - procedures
  - standards
  - maintenance
  - consumables
  - environment
  - security
- Development services:
  - market research
  - other research services
  - business analysis
  - specification
  - analysis
  - design
  - testing
  - pilots/prototypes
  - implementation
  - post-implementation reviews
- Creative services:
  - public relations
  - market research
  - concepts
  - scripts
  - pre-production
  - story boards

- pilots
- visual aids
- video
- cine
- audio
- personal computer presentations
- multi-media
- advertisements
- commercials
- media services
- post-production
- Equipment services:
  - provision
  - installation
  - maintenance
  - related ancillaries
    - peripheral equipment
    - software
    - consumables
  - software provision
  - software maintenance
  - development (see also development services)
  - security, backup
- Technical support services:
  - bespoke services
  - operational
  - quality control
  - information management
  - capacity management
  - security management
  - coordination of in-house suppliers
  - coordination of external suppliers
  - maintenance management
  - advice on selection of equipment
  - advice on selection of related tools
  - advice on selection of consumables
  - advice on selection of other commercial services
  - other consultancy services
- Problem management:
  - services covered
  - help desk (level 1)
  - second and higher levels of support
  - problem resolution objectives:
    - response time
    - time to fix
    - accuracy
    - effectiveness
  - escalation procedure

- Education and training services:
    - type of training:
        'live'
        distance learning
        subscription TV
        video
        interactive video
        computer-based
        textbooks/manuals
        on-the-job
    - service provider
    - customer
    - in-house:
        bespoke
        off-the-shelf
    - external
    - marketing and certification
    - training programmes and schedules
- Administrative services:
    - accounting and charging
    - leasing arrangements
    - equipment rental
    - software rental/royalties
    - organization and reporting lines
    - insurance/risk management
    - contract management

Workload

Background (routine production type) services:

- Daily volumes:
    - peak
    - average
    - over each regime
- Weekly/monthly volumes:
    - maximum
    - average
    - over each regime
- Forecast growth, peak and average over each regime over six months, one year and two years
- Workload above which service level will not be guaranteed

Real-time services:

- Hourly transaction volumes/arrival rates:
    - peak
    - average
    - over each regime
- Daily peaking
- Over each regime
- Total number of customers

- Total number of customers able to access the service simultaneously
- Forecast growth, peak and average over each regime over six months, one year, two years
- Workload above which service level will not be guaranteed

Workload on delivery mechanisms:

- Hourly volumes/arrival rates:
  - peak
  - average
  - over each regime
- Daily volumes:
  - peak
  - average
  - over each regime
- Total number of customers
- Number of simultaneous customers
- Forecast growth, peak and average over each regime over six months, one year, two years

Facilities management:

- Service hours
- Service level requirement (by use of other relevant sections of this checklist)
- Forecast growth, peak and average over each regime over six months, one year, two years

Development workload:

- Existing workload
- Human resource available (permanent and contract staff)
- Corporate plan (systems implications)
- Headcount restraints
- Resource forecasting methodology
- Development tools or standards
- Project management responsibilities (sponsor, client, executive)
- Project management methodologies
- Design standards
- Design methodologies
- Quality assurance and quality control standards
- Testing responsibilities
- Pilot/prototype responsibilities
- Documentation responsibilities
- Forecast growth, peak and average over each regime over six months, one year, two years
- List:
  - job priorities
  - resource requirements
  - implementation deadlines
  - project schedules

Equipment supply services:

- Existing resource requirement
- Daily peaks and average demand
- Weekly peaks and average demand
- Forecast growth, peak and average over each regime over six months, one year, two years

Technical support services:

- For each support service specify:
  - existing resource commitment
  - daily peaks and average demand
  - weekly peak and average demand
  - forecast growth, peak and average over each regime over six months, one year, two years

Problem management:

- Identify support services covered
- Existing workload
- Hourly volume – peak, average, over each regime
- Daily volume – peak, average, over each regime
- Number of help desk calls getting 'engaged' tone
- Prioritization procedure
- New applications scheduled to move from development to production
- Operating system upgrades scheduled
- Hardware changes scheduled
- Environmental changes scheduled
- Forecast growth, peak and average over each regime over six months, one year, two years

Education and training:

- Numbers for on-the-job training:
  - trainees
  - trainers
- Numbers for subscription TV training:
  - trainees
  - courses
- Numbers for video training:
  - trainees
  - courses
- Numbers for interactive video:
  - trainees
  - courses
- Numbers for computer-based training:
  - trainees
  - courses
- Numbers for 'classroom' training in-house:
  - trainees
  - tutors

- Numbers for external courses:
  - trainees
  - courses
- Numbers for prerequisite training:
  - trainees
  - courses
  - tutors
- Tutor/student ratio
- Hardware to student ratio:
  - optimum
  - maximum
- Frequency of training
- Structured training schedule
- Numbers for marking and certification:
  - trainees
  - tutors
  - courses
- Forecast growth, peak and average (e.g. from new service or new customers) over each regime over six months, one year, two years

Administrative services:

- For each service:
- existing resource commitment
- forecast requirement daily peak and average, weekly peak and average, by all regimes covered
- forecast growth peak and average (e.g. from new services or new customers) over each regime over six months, one year, two years

Response levels

Establish theoretical maximum throughput, and apply capacity and workload forecasts to this to establish theoretical response. The theoretical response can be refined and made more realistic by factoring in outage or reduction of service caused by staff sickness or other absence, equipment failure etc.

Background:

- Turnround – time elapsed between:
  - job start to job end
  - receipt of input to delivery of output
  - average times compared to targets and related to volume
- Compliance with schedules
- Number of deadlines missed

Real-time work:

- Response time for specified type of transaction or for baskets of transactions
  - within location of service provider
  - 'in the customer's hands'
- Percentage of transactions falling within specified response targets for each type of transaction
- Reduced response times related to increased transaction workload
- Response targets peak, average, for each regime

Delivery mechanisms:

- Response times
- Percentage of transaction falling within specified response
- Reduced response times related to targets for each type of transaction workload
- Response targets peak, average, for each regime
- Compliance with delivery targets and schedules to each location

Facilities management:

- Compliance with service hours
- Standard service response (by use of relevant sections of checklist)
- Response to *ad hoc* requirements

Development services:

- Delivery from development to production compared to project planned time-scale
- Backlog

Creative services:

- Delivery from job received to output completed against planned timescale
- Backlog

Equipment supply services:

- As for relevant sections of checklist

Background services:

- And real-time work
- Compliance with 'hours of business'
- Elapsed time from request for equipment to delivery and installation

Technical support services:

- Defined for each service
- Compliance with deadlines
- Service frequency compared to schedule
- Reaction time for new requests
- Reaction time for urgent requests
- Backlog

Problem management:

- Time to answer
- Time to respond
- Time to provide work-round
- Time to fix
- Escalation invocations
- Backlog

Education and training:

- Compliance with published training schedules
- Compliance with individual course timetable
- Lead time to initiate new courses

- Lead time to revise existing courses to reflect changes
- Backlog

Administrative services:

- Elapsed time to register new customers
- Elapsed time to give new customers access to services required
- Timeliness of provision of accounting information
- Elapsed time between customer request and completion of service provision
- Backlog

Accuracy
Accuracy targets would be aimed towards a zero-defect service.

Background jobs:

- Accuracy of input (ratio of errors to volume)
- Definition of customer/service provider accuracy responsibilities
- Conditions for free repeat of job because of inaccuracy or missing quality targets
- Number of free repeats
- Impact on response level if customer quality targets are not met
- Mean-time between operator errors during each regime
- Number of errors during each regime
- Mean-time between errors during each regime
- Number of 'patches' to the service (quick fixes to solve problems) by time
- Number of changes applied (by time)
- Frequency of consumable 'out of stock'

Real-time work:

- Error rate (ratio to volume)
- Number of and frequency of service outages from same cause

Delivery mechanisms:

- Incidence of outage of primary routes
- Number of losses in transit (ratio to traffic)
- Number of defects in transit (ratio to traffic)
- Frequency and number of misroutes
- Number and frequency of service outages from same cause

Facilities management:

- Mean-time between operator error during each regime
- Number of errors during each regime
- Mean-time between errors during each regime
- Number of 'patches' or 'quick fixes' applied (by time)
- Number of changes applied (by time)
- Select from other sections of accuracy checklist as appropriate

Development services:

- Mean-time between errors:
  - at specification
  - on testing
  - in pilot/prototype

- – in production
- – per measurable unit produced
- Number of errors:
  - – at specification
  - – in testing
  - – in pilot/prototype
  - – in production
  - – as ratio to volume of output
  - – per measurable unit produced
- Impact of errors
- Number of 'patches' or 'quick fixes' applied (by time)
- Number of requests for changes (by time)
- Number of changes applied (by time)

Creative services:

- Defect rate of output
- Effectiveness of output

Equipment services:

- Select relevant items from accuracy checklist section

Technical support:

- Mean-time between errors
- Number of errors
- Impact of errors
- Correctness of information
- Number of revisions of published information
- Number of reiterations
- Number and frequency of complaints
- Number of help desk calls on identical problems

Problem management:

- Correctness of information
- Completeness of information
- Number of customer repeat calls on same problem
- Number of help desk calls on identical problems

Education and training:

- Student assessment of course quality (course critique forms)
- Performance on any tests (before/after)
- Line management feedback on effectiveness of training
- Retraining level

Administrative services:

- Frequency and number of errors
- Number and frequency of iterations
- Number and frequency of complaints

Availability

Production services (background and real-time). For each service:

- Define 'business hours', 'normal working hours' or 'extended working hours' etc.
  - i.e. scheduled times of availability
- Define 'availability' to take account of part-crippled service
- Percentage scheduled availability 'in customer's hands' for each regime and at peak periods

Delivery mechanisms:

- As for background/production services

Facilities management:

- As for background/production services

Development services:

- Resource delivered compared to resource required by project plan
- Project duration

Creative services:

- As for development services

Problem management:

- Define whether 'availability' includes:
  - use of answerphones
  - use of voice response systems
  - use of bought-in services
- Define 'business hours' for
  - help desk
  - second and higher level support
- Actual availability compared to 'business hours'
- Escalation procedure

Technical support:

- Define 'business hours'
- Define cover arrangement for leave, sickness, etc.

Education and training:

- Define 'business hours'
- Course schedules and timetables
- Location of courses

Administrative services:

- Define 'business hours'
- Define cover arrangements for leave, sickness, etc.
- Define special arrangements for public holidays

Constraints

Dependency on:

- Internal supplier with whom no SLA exists

- External supplier with whom contract does not explicitly cover the SLA requirements
- Shared resources
- Business priorities remaining constant
- Customer priorities remaining constant
- Capacity plans being approved
- Manpower plans being approved
- Budget being approved
- Customer usage aligning with forecasts

Charging and recovery:

- Cost or profit centre?
- Cost notification, cost allocation or charge-out?
- Break-even or standard costing?

Charging definition:

- Resource units
- Workload units
- Business units
- Items to be included in charging:
  - equipment resources
  - people time
  - consumables
  - technical support
  - consultancy
  - bought-in services
  - profit

Demand management by pricing:

- Higher price for 'gold star' service (better quality)
- Higher price for 'express' service (quicker service)
- Higher price for peak service
- Higher price for higher workload (to discourage overload)
- Discount for higher workload (to encourage full utilization)
- Discount for non-peak time or for non-prime time regimes

Personnel incentives:

- Contracts of employment
- Definition of gross misconduct (i.e. firing offences)
- Job descriptions
- Performance related pay
- Management by objectives

Monitoring of performance against SLA:

- Responsibilities of:
  - service provider
  - the customer
  - co-responsibilities
  - arbitrator

- Define:
    - what is to be measured?
    - where it is to be measured?
    - what is the basis of measurement?
    - what source data is to be used?
    - what software or other tools are to be used?
    - what procedures are to be adopted?
    - what assumptions are made?
    - what reports will be produced?
        by what method?
        in what format?
        to whom?
        how often?

SLA review and renegotiation procedure

Appendix B: sample service level agreement and escalation procedure

This agreement is based on one designed for a commercial bureau service. It is therefore a more contractually structured document and contains more textual explanation than might be appropriate for an internal SLA. It was designed as much to protect the service provider as to guarantee service and has more 'get outs' than might be appropriate for an in-house SLA.

A marketing function was in place with the ABC Service together with customer account management. A customer group was established to provide strategic input and to review overall service needs and performance.

Account managers hold separate service review meetings with individual customers to discuss customer-specific issues.

Some detail (equipment etc.) has been omitted for brevity.

The agreement contains defined problem escalation procedures.

The holes in this SLA are easy to see, but in practice it worked effectively.

Service level agreement

1. Quality of the service

1.1 Introduction

The purpose of this agreement is to define the ABC Service targets that will be offered to customers and to define the usage forecasts of each customer.

1.2 Definitions (times are used as examples)

The ABC Service means all equipment used to provide a service to customers, the underlying support services which ensure that the equipment functions satisfactorily, and the ancillary support service provided directly to customers.

Normal working hours means the hours between 0900 hours and 1700 hours Monday to Friday excluding all public holidays.

Extended working hours means the hours between 0800 hours and 1900 hours Monday to Friday and 0900 hours and 1200 hours Saturdays (except public holidays).

Specialist shall mean any person qualified to take the appropriate action or to provide the appropriate advice in relation to service problems.

2. Equipment used to provide the service

To be defined

3. Scheduled availability

The service shall be available during normal working hours except for scheduled downtime needed for maintenance of equipment, maintenance of environmental plant, essential building work, operational maintenance and unavoidable outages.

Customers shall have access to schedules specifying the future availability of the service. The schedules will cover rolling four week periods. Normally, customers will be given at least two weeks' notice of changes in the scheduled availability of the service during normal working hours and one week's notice of other alterations to the scheduled availability of the service.

Present scheduled maintenance arrangements are as follows:

To be defined

The service shall ensure that, whenever possible, maintenance activities are scheduled to take place outside the normal working hours and that customers are given at least 48 hours notice of such activity.

4. Service availability

It is the objective that each customer of the service shall be able to process work for at least 99% of the monthly scheduled time in normal working hours and 90% during extended working hours.

The service shall exercise all reasonable endeavours to ensure that there will be no more than two service interruptions per week, during normal working hours, or one service interruption per week in extended working hours, measured on a rolling four weekly basis.

5. Customer support

A responsive help desk service shall be provided to all customers during normal working hours. Help desk staff shall provide assistance with all aspects of the service either directly or through specialists. Help desk staff shall be trained to resolve 60% of customer calls within five minutes and shall have direct access to more experienced staff.

Problems and requests for technical assistance received by the help desk shall be referred to an appropriate specialist (as defined in Schedule 1) within five minutes if the help desk is unable to resolve the problem. If a quick resolution is not achieved within approximately 30 minutes the customer account manager or specialist shall endeavour to contact the customer within 20 to 45 minutes to explain the corrective action or investigations to be carried out, possible means of circumventing the problem and the arrangements for informing the customer of progress. Further escalation procedures are given in Annex A.

Outside normal working hours the help desk telephone will be answered by an answerphone and responded to by the help desk who will call the customer at the start of the next working day.

The help desk telephone number is :————————————————————

The customer shall appoint a customer representative who will be the focus for dealings with the ABC Service. The ABC Service shall appoint a customer account manager who will be the focus for dealings with the customer.

Review meetings between the customer account manager and the customer representative will be held at intervals not exceeding three months.

6. Customer representative

The customer representative shall be:

Name:

Address:

Telephone: Fax:

Changes of customer representative shall be notified to the customer account manager by fax within 24 hours of the change. Correspondence from the ABC Service shall normally be directed to the customer representative.

7. Customer account manager

The customer account manager shall be:

Name:

Address:

Telephone: Fax:

Changes of customer account manager shall be notified to the customer representative by fax within 24 hours of the change. Correspondence from the customer shall normally be directed to the customer account manager.

8. Arbitration

In the event of any dispute, the customer group shall act as arbitrator.

9. Ancillary services

During normal working hours reports required by the customer shall be mailed to the customer's site within six hours of a request. Reports generated by 1400 hours shall be sent by first-class post the same day.

10. Administration services

Standard administrative requests shall normally be serviced within 24 hours.

Accounting information provided by the ABC Service will enable the customer to determine the usage at individual job level.

Accounting information will be produced weekly to show the customer's usage for the previous week.

11. Change control

The periods between changes to the ABC Service which may alter the customer interface shall normally be greater than six months.

Customers shall be informed at least one month in advance of plans for changes which may alter the customer interface.

Proposals for major changes in the support services shall be reviewed by the customer group at least one month in advance.

12. Training

All new customers shall be given appropriate basic training to a maximum of one tutor day for each new customer in the use of the ABC Service. The training shall be tailored to meet the requirement of the customer. Additional or advanced training courses shall be arranged on request. These will be subject to additional charges.

13. Documentation

All customers shall be supplied with a copy of the customer guide describing how to use the ABC Service. Customer guides shall be updated after every major change to the service products.

14. Security

The ABC Service shall be responsible for issuing each of their authorized users with a PIN and account number. Customers shall exercise all reasonable endeavours to preserve the security of the ABC service by not revealing the PIN to any other party.

15. Special requirements

All reasonable endeavours shall be made by the ABC Service to provide non-standard services requested by customers. The provision of such services shall be subject to an additional charge.

16. Customer satisfaction

The quality of the ABC Service to customers will depend on many factors, some of which cannot be readily quantified. The ABC service shall monitor customer satisfaction and measures shall be taken to address any deficiencies detected as soon as possible using the procedures outlined in this agreement. A formal customer satisfaction survey shall be conducted by the ABC Service once a year and the results published to customers.

17. Customer workload forecasts

Customers shall provide workload forecasts for jobs to be turned round during normal working hours and during extended working hours. These forecasts shall identify total workload, average workload and peak workload. The customer shall also define output requirements, response requirements and turnround deadlines. The ABC Service shall not be responsible for shortfalls in service if these targets are exceeded. The Customer's forecasts are attached at Annex B.

18. Duration of agreement

The agreement shall commence on_____
and be valid until _____
within which period it may be renegotiated by mutual agreement.

19. Invoicing and payment

The ABC Service shall invoice the customer at intervals of approximately four weeks in arrears for the services provided to the customer in the previous accounting period.

   Payment shall be made no later than 30 days from invoice date.

Accounting period to be defined

20. Force majeure

No failure or omission to carry out or observe any of the stipulations or conditions of this Agreement shall except as expressly provided to the contrary herein give rise to any claim against either party or be deemed to be a breach of this agreement if such failure or omission arises from any cause beyond the reasonable control of that party.

Signed:

Name:	Name:
Capacity:	Capacity:
ABC Service	**Customer**

Annex A: ABC Service service level agreement

1. Management agreement and escalation procedures

1.1 Customer group

Executive responsibility for ensuring the success of the ABC Service shall reside with the customer group (CG) comprising:

- manager of the ABC Service
- a representative of each customer.

The CG shall normally meet quarterly when it will receive reports from the ABC Service manager.

This CG may review and if necessary recommend changes to the ABC Service.

A meeting shall be held regularly to review the following aspects:

- medium and long-term plans for changes to equipment or services likely to impact customers;
- any major technical exercise related to the service level agreement and agreed priorities;
- requirements for new services;
- overall availability, response and job turnaround for customer work and overall performance against service level agreements;
- the escalation procedures and agree necessary changes.

An extraordinary meeting of the customer group may be called by any two members of it giving the other parties two weeks' notice.

1.2 Customer account manager

A customer account manager shall be allocated by the ABC Service for each customer. Customer account managers shall be responsible for ensuring that, whenever possible, the technical and service requirements of the customer are being met.

Each customer account manager shall be responsible for monitoring the quality of the service being provided to specified customers and for reporting any deficiencies to the ABC Service manager. The customer account manager shall be responsible for ensuring that the customer is appraised, during normal working hours, of plans for addressing critical and major problems (see problem management below). The customer account manager shall also be responsible for providing regular updates to customers on progress towards problem resolution.

1.3 Customer representative

Each customer shall appoint a customer representative who shall liaise with the customer account manager and advise the customer account manager of significant changes in usage forecasts, of changed or new service requirements, and who shall be the focal point for the escalation procedures.

1.4 Problem management

The ABC Service shall be responsible for ensuring that procedures are in place to ensure that the standards for customer care specified in the service level agreement are met.

Customers shall report any difficulties they are having with the ABC Service to the help desk which shall be responsible for attempting to resolve problems as specified in the service level agreement and for the initial classification of the problem as detailed below.

All problems (technical or otherwise) affecting customers shall be placed in one of the following categories according to its severity:

1.4.1 Critical problems

This category includes, but is not confined to, all problems which have an impact on the accessibility criteria defined in the service level agreement. In particular any problem which results in the loss of the ABC Service or prevents effective use of the ABC Service by the customer for more than two hours shall be deemed a critical problem. The help desk shall keep a log of all major actions taken by the ABC Service to resolve the problem.

1.4.2 Major problems

This category includes all problems with the ABC Service which prevent a customer from using the ABC Service effectively for more than one hour.

1.4.3 Minor problems

All other problems affecting the efficient use of the ABC Service.

During normal working hours the automatic escalation procedures specified in figures attached to this annex shall be followed.

Outside normal working hours, the ABC Service shall follow their standard escalation procedures to resolve problems. Additionally, the customer account manager shall be appraised of outstanding critical problems and major problems within two hours of the start of the next working day. Any problems which occur outside of normal working hours and which are not resolved by the next working day shall be subject to the escalation procedures specified in the figures attached.

All problems received during normal working hours by the ABC Service help desk which cannot be resolved within five minutes by the relevant help desk staff shall be referred to an appropriate specialist. However, the relevant help desk staff shall retain responsibility for ensuring that the customer is contacted within one hour of the initial call and that the appropriate escalation procedure is followed until the problem is solved or reported to the ABC Service manager. The ABC Service manager shall then assume responsibility for ensuring that the problem is resolved as quickly as possible. The appropriate customer account manager shall be responsible for keeping the customer informed of progress on a regular basis depending on the nature of the problem.

In some instances problems may initially be detected or reported to ABC Service staff other than those employed on the help desk. In these cases the aim is that the initial contact shall ensure that the problem is reported to the help desk as soon as possible.

Customer enquiries to the ABC Service help desk shall be logged. The entries in the logs for problems reported by customers shall record the time and date of the initial contact, the problem category, the action taken and the time when the problem was resolved to the said customer's satisfaction. The logs shall be processed periodically to extract information which would be useful in monitoring the quality of the ABC Service.

The ABC Service manager shall be informed immediately if any customer experiences more than one critical problem within a week, or if there is more than one major problem at any one time affecting a customer.

1.5 Monitoring procedures

The ABC Service manager or customer account manager shall regularly review outstanding problems with the ABC Service with the customer representative. A customer representative may call meetings with the ABC Service manager or customer account manager to review or resolve outstanding problems.

A quarterly meeting shall be held between the customer account manager and customer representative to review the routine performance of the ABC Service.

This 'service review meeting' shall be chaired by the customer account manager and, as necessary, representatives of each of the departments involved in the delivery of the ABC Service shall attend. The ABC Service provided to the customer shall be reviewed to ensure that the criteria in the service level agreement are being met.

The customer account manager shall use the information gathered at the service review meetings to develop plans for improving the ABC Service and ensuring that the line managers responsible for providing support services are appraised of potential problem areas.

Automatic escalation for critical problems
(during normal working hours)

Time elapsed since the initial report of the problem	Escalation level
Initial contact	
5 minutes	Appraise specialist
30 minutes	Escalate to customer account manager
1 hour	Review with appropriate line manager reporting to ABC Service manager
2 hours	Escalate to ABC Service manager

Automatic escalation for major problems
(during normal working hours)

Time elapsed since the initial report of the problem	Escalation level
Initial contact	
5 minutes	Appraise specialist
30 minutes	Escalate to customer account manager
1 hour	Review with appropriate line manager reporting to ABC Service manager
2 hours	Escalate to ABC Service manager

Automatic escalation for minor problems
(during normal working hours)

Time elapsed since the initial report of the problem	Escalation Level
Initial contact	
5 minutes	Appraise specialist
1 week	Inform customer account manager and appropriate line managers
Weekly review	

Automatic escalation for critical and major problems
(in extended working hours)

Time elapsed since the initial report of the problem	Escalation level
	Initial contact
5 minutes	Senior member of staff on extended working hours calls in maintenance as appropriate
1 hour	Advise appropriate line manager (if available) otherwise it is referred to ABC Service manager
Next working day	Advise ABC Service manager Advise customer account manager

2. Problem management: information to be maintained

Information which should be recorded by the problem management system should include the following basics:

- Customer details:
  - customer's name
  - telephone number
  - full address
  - how reported (e.g. telephone, fax)
- Problem description:
  - unique problem number
  - title of problem
  - customer's description of the problem
  - description of the current state of affairs
  - resolution of the problem
  - supplier reference (e.g. maintenance supplier)
  - estimated fix date and time

All the above should be date/time stamped.

- Priority:
  - initial priority
  - current priority
- ABC Service person handling the problem
- Subsequently, actual fix date and time.

Annex B: ABC Service service level agreement

1. Customer forecasts

To be defined

Appendix C: standard SLA

This SLA format may be suitable for in-house use.

This format results in a more compact and maintainable document concentrating on specific service objectives from the customer's perspective.

The SLA is then backed up by a comprehensive service guide containing descriptions and measurement criteria for the individual service products.

An outline for a service handbook or service guide is contained in Chapter 4. The service guide associated with this SLA could contain sections describing:

- equipment and service components
- service products
- general definitions (e.g. problem priorities)
- processes (e.g. problem management, help desk, escalation procedures, charging) with each service product specified in terms of:
  - description
  - person/group accountable
  - criteria for measuring availability
  - criteria for measuring response.

Service level agreement

Date:
Ref:

FOR THE   SERVICE

(a) **The Agreement**

Period of agreement:
  From: To:

Review date:

Covering:

- Description and scope of service
- Availability – hours of service
- Recovery from loss of service
- Performance – response time and turnround
- Standard terms and conditions
- Non-standard variations for this agreement

Agreed by	Service owner	Customer representative	Service supplier
Department	_____	_____	_____
Signature	_____	_____	_____
Date	_____	_____	_____

(b) **Description and scope of service**

Points of service delivery are:

(c) **Availability**

Service regimes

(1) Normal working hours:

Days of week etc.	Hours (from–to)	Guarantee level (if non-standard)

(2) Extended working hours

Days of week etc.	Hours (from–to)	Guarantee level (if non-standard)

(3) Others:

Days of week etc.	Hours (from–to)	Guarantee level if non-standard)

Availability targets (in guaranteed periods only):

	Monthly average	13 week rolling average
Delivery point 1:		
Delivery point 2:		
End to end:		

Service interruptions per week – maximum:

(d) **Recovery from loss of service**

Target recovery time (hours):

Maximum processing loss (working hours):

(e) **Performance (figures refer to peak hours)**

Transaction or job categories:

	Description	Throughput limits
1.		
2.		
3.		
4.		

Performance targets (for each category):

	Average response of turnround	Percentage less than	Maximum volume/hour
1.			
2.			
3.			
4.			

Points of measurement of response time are:

(f) **Customer Support Levels**

Problems, queries and requests for help or information must be made to the service desk on extension 111. The service desk will be staffed from 0800 hours to 1800 hours each working day.

Working calls to the service desk must be made only by customer representatives.

Where the service desk cannot resolve a problem within five minutes it will be directed to the appropriate technical support specialist. The customer will be advised by the service desk as soon as a solution is found, or kept informed of progress in accordance with standard escalation procedures laid down in the service guide.

Target fault resolution times are as follows:

Priority level	Time (hours)
A	1
B	2
C	Same working day
D	Next working day
E	Within 3 working days

(g) **To comply with the SLA, error levels must fall below the following maximum**

Priority level	Number
A	1
B	2
C	8
D	15
E	20

(h) **Change control procedures**

Change control procedures to be followed as follows:

(j) **Business continuity**

Business continuity plans to be implemented in the event of disaster are as follows:

(k) **Service review**

Service review meetings will be held monthly and both parties to the agreement will be represented. The purpose of these meetings is to:

- review service achievements against SLA targets for the previous month
- identify problems and trends
- identify new requirements and changes
- undertake action to improve SLA compliance or review SLA target.

(l) **Service guide**

Service guide distribution is as follows:

Arrangements for making changes to the service guide are defined in the service guide.

(m) **Growth forecasts**

1. Real-time jobs

2. Background jobs

(n) **Restrictions**

The following restrictions apply to this service level agreement:

(p) **Security**

The following security requirements apply:

(q) **Standard terms and conditions**

(1) Standard procedures will apply to all services unless otherwise stated. These cover change control, acceptance, problem management, customer liaison, work scheduling, capacity planning, security and charging. Details are contained in the service guide.

(2) Monitoring of the agreement will be against the targets specified in this SLA. Reporting will be monthly to the signatories or their nominees.

(3) The agreed availability targets are used by the service to determine the amount of support required.

(4) Standard charges, escalation procedures and contacts are set out in the service guide, as are general service standards, definitions and explanatory notes on the SLA process and completion of this form.

(r) **Non-standard variation for this Agreement**

(e.g. special charges or contacts)

(s) **Changes to the SLA**

Procedures for requesting changes to the SLA are detailed in the service guide.

Bibliography

Barham, W. J. and Murrey Faithfull (1988) Service level management at Lloyds Bank, *Conference Proceedings of UK Computer Measurement Group (CMG)* pp. 577–82.

Chapman, C.D., Ward, S.C. and McDonald, M. (undated) *Roles, Responsibilities and Risks in Management Contracts*, Science and Engineering Research Council, Swindon.

Clifford-Winters, T. (1986) Service level agreements: to negotiate or impose, *Conference Proceedings of UK CMG*, May, pp. 37–59.

Dugmore, J. (1989) Managing the gap between service targets and actual performance, *Conference Proceedings of UK CMG*, June, pp. 259–64, and (1990) *Conference Proceedings of SHARE Europe*, April, pp. 551–2.

Elliot, T. (1990) Pitfalls and joys of service level agreements, *Conference Proceedings of SHARE Europe*, April, pp. 501–9.

Georgopoulos, B.S. (1973) An open system theory model for organizational research, in Negandhi, A.R. (ed.), *Modern Organization Theory*, Kent State University Press, Ohio.

Hiles, A. (1991) *The Complete Guide to IT Service Level Agreements*, Elsevier, Oxford.

Miller, G. W. A. (1988) Service level agreements: good fences makes good neighbours, *Conference Proceedings of CMG*, pp. 1–21.

Propst, J. W. (1985) Developing effective service level agreements, *Conference Proceedings of CMG*, December, pp. 704–9.

Rene, J. (1990) Service level agreements: practical implementation, *Conference Proceedings of CMG*, May.

Sherkow, A. M. (1986) Using service level objectives, *Conference Proceedings of CMG*, December, pp. 623–8.

Wenk, D. (1985) Management control of management information systems, *Conference Proceedings of CMG*, December, pp. 486–9.

ISO International Standards

ISO 8402: 1986, *Quality – Vocabulary*.

ISO 9000: 1987, *Quality management and quality assurance standards – guidelines for selection and use*.

ISO 9001: 1987, *Quality systems – model for quality assurance in design/development, production, installation and servicing*.

ISO 9002: 1987, *Quality systems – model for quality assurance in production and installation*.

ISO 9003: 1987, *Quality systems – model for quality assurance in final inspection and test*.

ISO 9004: 1987, *Quality management and quality system elements – guidelines*.

ISO Draft International Standards

ISO/DIS 9004–2, *Quality management and quality system elements – Part 2: Guidelines for services.*

ISO/DIS 10011, *Generic guidelines for auditing quality systems.*

Index